TRUST IN THE LORD

Letting the Spirit Be Your Guide

Diane Bills

Covenant Communications, Inc.

Trust in the Lord: Letting the Spirit Be Your Guide
Published by Covenant Communications, Inc.
American Fork, Utah
© 1996 by Diane Bills
Printed in the United States of America
First printing August 1996

01 00 99 98 97 96   10 9 8 7 6 5 4 3 2 1
ISBN 1-55503-983-9

Cover Painting by Robert Barrett

Dedication

I dedicate this work to Him . . . He who lives perfectly, gives perfectly, loves perfectly, and cares perfectly. He is the one we can always and very personally trust.

ACKNOWLEDGMENTS

My heartfelt thanks goes to Arlene Bascom, who carefully edited and organized my writing. Also warmest thanks to JoAnn Jolley at Covenant Communications and others in her charge for their valuable contributions. And finally, I genuinely appreciate the encouragement, kindness, love, and patience of my family as I have worked many long hours on this project.

CONTENTS

FOREWORD

Somewhere between seven and ten years ago, I was in the Jordan River Temple and had a sweet, sweet experience. While sitting in the celestial room, I offered a silent prayer, asking Heavenly Father what He would desire me to do. As I waited and listened, impressions came distinctly into my mind. I was to write a book—a book on faith. The contents of the book came to me clearly, as well as its title: *Trust in the Lord.* I was overcome with tender feelings, and overwhelmed that He wanted *me* to write a book.

I have never considered myself a writer, although I enjoy writing. I have done extensive speaking, but writing and speaking are quite different. With a busy life and young children at home, I put the project on a back burner. As time passed, I attempted to co-author two separate books on completely different subjects. My thinking was that these projects would prepare me to write the book on faith. Neither of the books came to fruition. It was only when I began to write what I had been told to write that the puzzle pieces fell perfectly into place. Line upon line, I was guided through this project and filled with an outpouring of the Spirit. I have also been led to editors, resource people, and others who have made valuable contributions to this endeavor.

A few years ago, when the book was nearly finished, I became a single parent. I was so overcome with grief that I shelved the book and determined that that was where it would stay. I was going through my own personal "Gethsemane," and I couldn't even think of continuing my work. It was, however, a time during which the message to "Trust in the Lord" became the overwhelming essence of my life. On two separate occasions I received distinct spiritual promptings to "finish the book." And so, humbly, I did.

I have prayed throughout my life that I might be an instrument in the Lord's hands. Perhaps, in some small way, this book will be a vehicle to do that. It is my sincere prayer that there may be a thought, a scripture, or an experience found herein that is personally for you . . . from Him.

Diane Bills

Chapter One

SONS AND DAUGHTERS OF A HEAVENLY KING

As a student at the University of Utah, I served on the student council for the LDS Institute of Religion. One weekend a group from the council drove together to a leadership conference in Park City. As we drove, I had an interesting conversation with Lee Yates, the council president. Lee asked me, "Diane, what do you think motivates people?"

I thought for a few minutes and then gave him what I thought were some respectable answers.

Lee looked at me and said, "Good answers, but I've discovered one thing that motivates people even more than those . . . so much so, I believe it is the number-one motivator of people." He continued, "On your committee you have some people you could call and ask to do something and it would be handled. There are others who come up with one excuse after another. Why is that?"

"I'm not sure," I said. "Please tell us!" His answer was simple yet profound. The answer would eventually change my life. I spent a period of time studying the concept, and have since then traveled all over this nation teaching it.

Lee Yates felt, and I came to believe, that what motivates people most is their *self-esteem*—the way they feel about themselves.

Who do you know who is accomplishing admirable goals? Can you guess how such people feel about themselves most of the time? They like themselves! Because they do, they are motivated to achieve worthwhile goals. People who feel good about themselves are the ones who make things happen in life.

All of us have days when we don't feel like facing the world. What would it take for us to feel so good every day that we would look forward to facing every aspect of our lives, no matter what outside pressures we had, what stresses we were under, or what challenges and trials we were going through?

There is a key to feeling good inside. Some have discovered it, but many have not. I believe this key lies in seeing ourselves as God sees us and basing our worth on who we really are. This spiritual insight can give us a foundation to help us meet any challenge in life with confidence.

As I have traveled around the country teaching self-esteem, I have learned that we usually base our feelings of self-worth on how we think other people see us.

Let me share with you a simple story that illustrates this. When I was twelve years old, just entering the awkward years, I unknowingly looked the part. I had short, cropped-off hair, freckles, protruding teeth, black-rimmed glasses, long skinny legs, and big feet! I was even jokingly given the nickname "Beanpole Legs."

In spite of my awkwardness, my mother repeatedly told me I was beautiful. Amazingly, I believed her! I didn't know I was funny-looking. Mom made positive comments to me daily during those transitional years. I remember feeling good inside most of the time. I would go outside to play with my friends and then come home for a while, where Mom would build me up. I would then run back out to meet my world with confidence.

It wasn't until I was about seventeen or eighteen that I made the surprising discovery that I had been awkward-looking at twelve. I would look at the family picture albums and laughingly say, "Hey, Mom, you used to tell me I was really cute—but look at these pictures!" Mom would just smile and nod.

I realize now that my mother was able to look beyond the outward awkwardness of a young twelve-year-old. She looked inside her daughter and saw beauty, and she sincerely reflected that to me often. Now, many years later, I often thank Mom for doing that for me. She gave me a great gift.

It is common to place our worth on things outside ourselves.

Years ago, I found myself doing just that. Yet because of this tendency, I had an experience that opened my eyes, changed my life, and taught me a lot about self-worth.

When I was in high school, I wanted to become the queen of something—of anything! As insignificant as it seems now, it was important to me then. My cousins were all queens of something. One cousin even went on to the Miss America pageant.

One of my closest cousins, Cami, was my age. She and I spent a lot of time together as we were growing up. When we became teenagers, it seemed as though she was always winning some pageant or other. I wasn't envious of my cousin; I was excited every time she won. But I longed to have a similar experience myself.

After we graduated from high school, Cami and I were roommates at Brigham Young University for several years. Toward the end of our sophomore year, BYU announced the biggest queen pageant the school had ever had. The winner, the "Centennial Belle of the Y," would get a full-ride scholarship and become the school's official hostess, meeting with and escorting any dignitaries who visited the BYU campus.

Now, men may relate better to this honor if they imagine trying out for a Centennial All-Star Basketball Team, with one young man chosen as BYU Athlete of the Year, to receive a full-ride scholarship and be the official school athlete who would welcome all other coaches, teams, or athletes who visited the campus.

I was thrilled about such an opportunity, and I definitely wanted to get involved. When I checked the contest's requirements, I found, to my dismay, that the competition was going to last five weeks. Five weeks! I belonged to a singing and dancing group that had practiced all year for a spring tour that would begin in only four weeks. I was extremely disappointed that I wouldn't be able to participate in the contest.

My cousin came home from school that same day bubbly and excited, announcing that she was going to enter the contest.

"You're so lucky," I said. "I would love to enter, but I can't because the contest lasts five weeks, and our singing group is going on tour in four weeks."

Cami encouraged me to enter the contest anyway. "We can make lots of friends and see how far we can go. We probably won't make it that far anyway."

She's right, I thought. It would be fun—especially if we did it together. "Let me think about it," I said. I decided to pray about it and follow my feelings. As I prayed I felt a sweet peace inside.

"Sign me up—I'm in!" I told her. Cami was pleased with my decision.

The contest began with approximately 130 young women. Each week there would be some sort of competition. The judges would keep an overall running score for each girl. Each week, some girls would be cut from the competition, and those with the highest scores would continue to compete. After the final cut to five girls, the BYU student body would vote for the winner, and the four others would be her attendants.

The first competition was in modeling, poise, and posture. After the competition I felt sure I hadn't made it. I didn't even want to look at the board with the list of winners. Cami hurried home from school to tell me we were both on the list. I was shocked! Her name appeared in the campus newspaper as one of the top three for that segment of the competition.

The second part of the contest involved baking a cake from scratch and making an article of clothing or a craft project of our choosing. Once again, at the end of the competition, my name was on the posted list!

In the third competition, we had to write and give a ten-minute speech about BYU, as well as an impromptu speech. The most surprising news came when my name appeared in the newspaper as one of the top three for that competition. I consequently made the third cut—to twenty-five girls.

The fourth part of the contest was the part we all dreaded most—four in-depth, one-on-one interviews about art, literature, music, philosophy, and religion.

That Saturday morning we were all uptight about the interviews. Just before they began, I asked myself why I was so nervous. After all, it was the end of the fourth week of competition. My singing group was going on tour in two days. The contest was basically over for me. I reasoned that I might as well go to the interviews and have fun.

When we arrived, I found myself cheering everyone else on. As I was interviewed I felt totally relaxed, even laughing and joking with the interviewers. At this point I wasn't nervous because it didn't matter how well I did.

As soon as we were through, I went to the woman who was in charge of the contest and told her I was going to have to drop out because I would be leaving to go on tour on Monday, explaining that I hadn't expected to make it that far. She was surprised I couldn't finish the contest. She said, "Let me just go see how you did today."

She left to meet with the judges and was gone for what seemed an eternity. She came back through the door, looked at me, and said, "Don't go on tour."

"But I *have* to," I answered.

She repeated, "Don't go on tour."

"You don't understand," I said. "I'm in a singing and dancing group, and we are leaving on tour in two days!"

"Diane, I shouldn't tell you this, but today you got the top score on the interviews."

"I *what?*"

"You got the top score on the interviews. Because of today's score, you are now in first place in the overall cumulative score of the contest. You've made it! Right now you are practically guaranteed to make it into the royalty. Just stay until Tuesday night to do your talent, then fly out and meet your singing group on Wednesday."

I stood there in shock. "I can't believe this!" I said. I tried to be calm, but my insides were in a jumble.

"I'll be there Tuesday night," I said. "You can count on it! I'll do whatever it takes to be there."

I ran to my tour director's house, about a mile off-campus, and explained to him my dilemma. We tried to figure out a way for me to stay until Tuesday night and fly out to meet our group on Wednesday. As we looked at the tour itinerary, we realized the group would not be near an airport on Wednesday.

"It won't work," he said. "There is no way we can come to get you at any of these airports. They are hours away." Nevertheless, he sensed my intense desire to complete the contest and finally told me I could stay home from tour and finish the competition.

"Thank you, thank you, thank you," I said.

As he walked me to the door, he paused and said, "Wait a minute. There's something I hadn't even considered. What about your partner? If you stay, your partner and the couple opposite you on stage won't be able to perform."

We both stopped. I had forgotten that everything our group did was symmetrical, and there was no backup to take my place.

"You can still stay for the contest, Diane. But if you do, be aware that those three people won't be able to perform," he said. "I'll let you make the decision."

What a dilemma! I didn't know what to do. So I did the logical thing—I called my parents and asked them what to do! They were pleasantly surprised that I had made it into the finals, and they told me to come home to Salt Lake City so we could talk.

Dad and Mom were waiting with open arms when I arrived. We laughed, cried, and talked, desperately trying to figure out a way for me to finish the contest and still go on tour. Each solution we came up with wouldn't work for one reason or another, and we kept coming to a dead end.

Mom finally said, "We can't make this decision for you. However, I would suggest you talk to the one person who *can* give you the guidance you need."

Mom was right. I needed to talk with Heavenly Father. He would let me know what to do. I went into my bedroom and got on my knees to pray. I truly wanted an answer and decided I would pray until I got one.

Nothing happened at first. I prayed for a while longer, and still nothing happened. I continued to pray and wondered why, when I badly needed an answer, I was not receiving one.

If our Heavenly Father cares for us, why does he seem to withhold answers when we feel we need them most? Perhaps in his wisdom he knows a better way or time to give us an answer. It may be that we aren't asking for what is best for us at that moment in time, or possibly we're not listening well enough when the answer comes. Often, we need to humble ourselves more.

With still no answer, I began to pray with deeper intent and a more tender heart. I shared with my Heavenly Father all my feelings. I told him that I had always wanted to be a queen of something, and how I would feel good inside if only . . . As I humbled myself, I wept and prayed on. I don't recall how long my prayer lasted. I do know I had never prayed with such intent and humility.

The answer finally did come later that evening. It was clear, it was sweet, and it was complete. I knew Heavenly Father's will for me without question.

The following Monday morning I was on a bus headed for California. I dropped out of the contest, and my cousin went on to make it into the royalty. But I had received a most wonderful answer to my prayer. For a brief moment that evening, Heavenly Father let me know who I was. He let me feel in my heart that I didn't need to be the Centennial Belle to feel good about myself. He let me know that I was already a queen in his sight.

It is because of the answer that I share this story with you. For you see, the answer isn't just about me. It is also about you. We are all sons and daughters of a Heavenly King, and are heirs to all that he has. In a tender, spiritual way, that night he let me understand what he has in store for each of us—you and me—if we live worthily.

Those few brief moments of spiritual understanding in a quiet bedroom on a Saturday evening changed my life. The feelings of self-worth that swelled up inside me were indelibly imprinted upon my heart.

After that experience, I felt better about myself than if I had been crowned the Centennial Queen of BYU or been elected BYU's student body president. I learned there is not an award, an honor, a presidency, or a title that man can bestow that even compares with what God has in store for each of us.

I discovered that self-esteem doesn't come from being popular in the world, but from God. Feelings of worth are not measured by how we look or dress, or by the car we drive, the house we live in, the position or titles we hold, or the income we make. True self-worth comes from drawing close to God. It comes from building a true relationship with Heavenly Father, and in coming to see ourselves as he sees us.

Unfortunately, people sometimes get caught up in basing their self-esteem on what the world finds important. The following analogy, written by Sydney J. Harris, describes this tendency:

> The personality of man is not an apple that has to be polished, but a banana that has to be peeled. And the reason we neither communicate nor interact in any real way is that most of us spend our lives in polishing rather than peeling. Man's lifelong task is simply one, . . . to get rid of the "Persona" that divides his authentic self from the world. This persona is like the peeling on a banana: . . . something built up to protect from bruises and injury. The "authentic personality" knows that he is like a banana, . . . only as he peels himself down . . . can he reach out and make contact with his fellows. Most of us, however, think in terms of the apple, . . . We spend our lives in shining the surface, in making it rosy and gleaming, in perfecting the "image". . . . Almost everything in modern life is devoted to the polishing process, and little to the peeling process. It is the surface personality that we work on—the appearance, the clothes, the manners, the selling of the package, not the product. (Sydney J.

Harris, columnist for the *Chicago Sun Times*, quoted in
a sacrament meeting talk. Exact source unknown.)

As we work on polishing that outside image, we may say
things like: "I would feel so good about myself if I had a better job
or a big raise, or if I owned my own company. I would feel good
about myself if I could just get married . . . or if my marriage were
better. . . . I would feel good if we could just have a child. I would
feel great if we had a nicer home, a more manicured yard, a better automobile, an RV, a boat, or a summer home. I would feel
good about myself if I had more friends . . . or if my children had
more friends. I would feel great if my son could make the basketball team, or if my daughter were a cheerleader. I would feel good
if I were called to an important calling in the Church . . . or if I
had a college degree. I would feel good about myself if I could lose
weight (or gain it) . . . if I weren't going gray . . . if I didn't have
to wear these glasses . . . and on and on and on.

What really matters, as Alma says, are not these things. He
asks: "Have ye received his image in your countenances?" (Alma
5:14). As we discover who we really are and receive the Lord's
image in our countenances, a miracle takes place in our spirits. No
longer do we need possessions or degrees to feel good about ourselves. No longer are we cliquish in neighborhoods or wards. No
longer do we have a desire to speak unkindly, to spurn a neighbor,
or to gossip. We have no desire to leave anyone out or put anyone
down—including ourselves. How could we? We and they are
cherished sons or daughters of God.

As we discover who we are, we lose any desire to do evil. We
only want to do righteous things. What the world says and does
no longer matters. Instead of craving the "image of the world,"
our hearts begin to focus on having the "image of Christ" in our
countenances.

Our hearts fill with charity when we truly know who we are.
Our lives become centered in service. We desire only to do good
for ourselves and others. Like Enos of old, we begin to have a

desire to pray for ourselves, our families and friends, and even our enemies.

Knowing who we are is central to self-esteem. One day a religion professor at BYU and his son were driving together in the car. As they drove past a certain house, his son pointed it out and, full of exuberance, said, "Dad, see that house? The son of the prophet, President Benson, lives there. Isn't that neat?"

The father looked at his son and asked, "Whose son are you?"

The son answered, "Well, Dad, I'm your son. You're cool and all, but the man who lives there is the son of the *prophet of God!*"

The professor asked him again, "Son, whose son are *you*? Quietly and soberly, the son replied, "Oh, you mean God's son."

"Yes, I mean God. You are a son of God."

I am reminded of a popular song from the Latter-day Saint play, *Saturday's Warrior*. In it, a confused young man sings,

> *I take some paper in my hand*
> *And with a pencil draw a man,*
> *The dream of what I'd really, really like to be.*
> *A man with courage in his brow,*
> *Who's licked his doubts and fears somehow.*
> *A warrior of great nobility. But who am I? . . .*

That is the question each of us needs to ask ourselves and find the answer to: Who am I?

In a talk I heard many years ago, a mission president's wife told of a time when she and her husband were presiding over a mission in the Eastern States. She was given the opportunity to speak to the missionaries at a conference, and she wanted to give them a message that would help them meet their challenges. She prayed about the assignment, but no idea came. She prayed even more diligently, but still she received no inspiration. As the day approached for the conference, she still didn't know what to speak about. The day before the conference she began a fast, hoping that some inspiration would come soon. She fasted for many hours and poured her heart out in prayer—still no answer.

The day of the conference came. This sister dressed for the conference, praying all the while, with still no idea about what she would say.

The mission president's quarters were upstairs, above the room where the missionaries would congregate. As she and her husband walked toward the steps leading into the room where the missionaries were assembled, with all her heart this humble sister pleaded with Heavenly Father to help her know what he would have her say to the missionaries.

At the moment she and her husband began to descend the steps, a voice spoke clearly to her mind, saying, "Tell them who they are—tell them they are my royal sons and daughters."

This sister walked into the mission conference that day and delivered a powerful message to the missionaries from their Father in Heaven, telling them who they were.

Many of his sons and daughters do not know who they are. Do you see yourself as God sees you? Do you see your potential and what God wants you to become?

Brother Verl Asay, a much-loved seminary teacher at Olympus Junior High School in Salt Lake City, was a kind and gentle man who had been called to be a stake patriarch at the age of thirty-six and had been a patriarch for many years. One day he was scheduled to address all the seminary classes. He had a reputation as a spiritual giant, and the students were eager to hear him.

That day when Brother Asay walked into the classroom, there were tears in his eyes. "Today, my young friends," he said, "I have had one of the most spiritual experiences of my life. As you came up the steps into the building, the Lord lifted the veil from my eyes and let me see who you are."

A hush came over the students as they felt a sweet spirit in the room. Then came words they would never forget. Brother Asay said, "I felt as though I wanted to bow down before you. . . ." Tears filled the students' eyes. This man, their leader and their friend, had had the privilege of seeing their spirits—of experiencing their true worth, and he shared it with them.

Prayer is an important part of this process of learning to understand who we are. While I was attending college at BYU, I took a religion class from Brother George Pace. During the beginning weeks of that class, Brother Pace challenged each of us to make our prayers more meaningful. Instead of getting on our knees in the morning and at night and saying a "quickie" routine prayer, he encouraged us to take the time each day to offer a prayer that lasted at least fifteen minutes.

He challenged all of us to say that kind of prayer for thirty days. It wasn't an assignment; no one would be graded. But Brother Pace told us that if we would fulfill that challenge for one month, it would change our lives.

I remember thinking, "Wow, what a wonderful promise. I'm going to accept that challenge." For the first few days, I did. Then I got busy with the routine of schoolwork and outside activities. I found myself once again saying my "quickie" prayers. Somehow, I let the opportunity to make my prayers more meaningful pass me by.

At the end of that month, Brother Pace invited those who had accepted the challenge to bear their testimonies. One by one, they stood and bore testimony of how their lives had been changed. I felt envious and disappointed that I hadn't paid the price to have a real life-changing experience with prayer. Now, one would think that at that point, I would go ahead and begin to make more time for prayer on my own, but I didn't. My life was busy, and I let time pass.

At the beginning of the next semester, as I was sitting in part two of that class, Brother Pace once again gave the class the prayer challenge. This time I decided I would not let this opportunity pass me by again.

Every day I made it a point to pray for at least fifteen minutes. It was really hard at first. I wasn't accustomed to praying that long. I ran out of things to say, and I felt I didn't have the time to pray so long. But I did not give up.

I testify to you that that experience *did* change my life. During that time I learned more about prayer and about myself than in all the previous years of my young life.

As we make prayer one of the central parts of our day, God will let us know, feel, and understand things about ourselves. Each day he will strengthen us. We will be filled with the Spirit. Line upon line and precept upon precept, he will let us know who we are in his sight and what we can become.

From that point on, I chose to make prayer one of the most important parts of my day. It was difficult to find a quiet spot in my apartment with people coming and going at all waking hours. So I decided to find a quiet spot on campus where I would go each day and sit, look at the mountains, and pray in my heart.

Many spiritual insights come when a person takes time in meaningful daily prayer. Perhaps each of us could find a quiet spot to retire to sometime during a day, during our lunch hour at work or while the children are napping. The location isn't important. It could be on a front or back porch, in a quiet spot on a school campus, in a backyard, on a park bench, in an office, car, or bedroom, or, as the scriptures suggest, in our closets. It can be in any place where we can sit or kneel and truly pour out our hearts in prayer for at least fifteen minutes a day. Prayer is the key to knowing who we are and what God expects of us.

Our elder brother, Jesus Christ, beautifully illustrated this principle by example: "And when he had sent the multitudes away, he went up into a mountain apart to pray: and when the evening was come, he was there alone" (Matt. 14:23).

Jesus often retired by himself into the wilderness, where he spent hours in prayer. In this way he gained a perfect understanding of who he was and what his purpose was:

> For he whom God hath sent speaketh the words of God: for God giveth not the Spirit by measure unto him. The Father loveth the Son, and hath given all things into his hand (John 3:34-35). . . .

> Then cried Jesus in the temple as he taught, saying,
> Ye both know me, and ye know whence I am: and I am
> not come of myself, but he that sent me is true, whom
> ye know not. But I know him: for I am from him, and
> he hath sent me (John 7:28-29).

Throughout his life, Jesus was treated cruelly by many jealous religious leaders. Some did everything they could to destroy him. It didn't matter what anyone said or did to Jesus; his relationship with his Father was complete and secure. Jesus said, "I know him . . ." (John 7:29). Jesus did know his Father. He went to his Father often in prayer.

God is our Father also. We are all sons and daughters of a Heavenly King. We are heirs to all that he has. He loves us tenderly, as a father loves his children. Do we go to him often and pour out our hearts in prayer? Do we honestly pay the price to understand more fully who we are?

As it was with Jesus, Joseph Smith, and others, it can be for us. When life seems difficult and the world seems cruel, when others hurt or betray us or tempt or harm us, we will still feel good about ourselves if we have learned to turn to the true source of strength. We can turn humbly to our Heavenly Father in prayer. He knows and loves us and will help us to meet our challenges. As Alma states, "I do know that whosoever shall put their trust in God shall be supported in their trials, and their troubles, and their afflictions, and shall be lifted up at the last day" (Alma 36:3).

True feelings of worth come from developing a close relationship with our Father in Heaven and his Son. Through prayer, we can come to more fully understand who we are and God's purposes for us.

Abraham, Moses, Nephi, Alma, and others who have gone before us have discovered this marvelous secret, as did Joseph Smith. When we understand this principle, it becomes easier to understand how Joseph Smith could be persecuted and harassed so often and yet always stay firm in the faith. Over a period of time, through prayer and revelation, he came to understand who he was and what Heavenly Father would have him do in his life.

The Doctrine and Covenants tells us,

> Behold, thou wast *called and chosen* to write the Book of Mormon, and to my ministry; and I have lifted thee up out of thine afflictions, and have counseled thee, that thou has been delivered from all thine enemies, and thou has been delivered from the powers of Satan and from darkness! (D&C 24:1; italics added)

Many times during Joseph Smith's life, people who had once been close to him abandoned him, calling him a fallen prophet. Even some of those who had served with him in high places in the Church apostatized because of jealousy or sin, then turned on Joseph in an effort to justify their actions. I'm sure such problems were painful for the Prophet to face, but others' actions did not affect how he felt about himself. Joseph had built a strong relationship with God through prayer. He understood that true feelings of worth don't come from peers, but from God.

I have heard it said, "We are not human beings here to have a spiritual experience, but rather, we are spiritual beings here to have a human experience." (Quoted by Brenda Hales, Relief Society General Board member, in a sacrament meeting. Original source unknown.) At times, mortality can seem like awkward years to our spirits, which are accustomed to the spirit world we just left.

Just as when I was an awkward twelve-year-old who would go home often to be with my mother so she could build me up, we, too, can go home often to our parent—our Heavenly Parent—in prayer, and listen as he builds us up. Then we can go forth with courage, facing the world and the challenges of our lives with confidence.

Chapter Two

TRUSTING IN THE LORD

Trust in the Lord with all thine heart; and lean not unto thine own understanding. In all thy ways acknowledge him, and he shall direct thy paths. (Proverbs 3:5-6)

This scripture has been a favorite of mine since the late 1970s. In the summer of 1976, my friend Debbie and I enjoyed participating in the cast of the Hill Cumorah Pageant. As we traveled home together after the pageant on a large Trailways bus, our thoughts were focused on another subject. My missionary boyfriend was coming home in two weeks, and Debbie's missionary was coming home shortly thereafter. Debbie and I had known our boyfriends for several years. We had dated them in high school and college. After just a few more weeks, we would be together with them again. We felt excitement and anticipation about seeing them. What would they be like? Would we still feel the same about each other? How soon would we each be getting married? We talked about our ideas, wedding plans, and trousseaus for hours as the bus made its way across the country back to Utah.

The days and weeks went by swiftly. Soon the young man I hoped to marry was standing in front of me. The relationship seemed wonderful at first as we shared experiences we had each had over the past few years, laughed and cried together, and talked about things that were meaningful and spiritual.

After we had been together for several days, however, my dream began to fade. He came to see me often; yet each time we were together, something deep down inside held me back from him. What was it? Was I just frightened? I couldn't understand what was happening. I cared about him, but I had an uneasy feeling that he wasn't my eternal companion.

My boyfriend could sense that something was wrong. He told me the sparkle had gone out of my eyes. He questioned me several times, and I told him how confused I was feeling, but that I didn't know the reason. I was unsure of my feelings and frightened. I said, "Just give me more time. I'm sure the feelings will go away."

I was starting to sense that at times he, too, was feeling uneasy about our relationship. I didn't know what to do.

Debbie's boyfriend had also come home from his mission, and very soon they were engaged. Things fell easily into place for them, while things were falling out of place for me. Debbie's dream was coming true, and mine was shattering.

I was attending the University of Utah at the time. My returned missionary was planning to go back to BYU in January, but he stayed home in Salt Lake that fall semester to work and to make it easier for us to be together.

I had found a special spot on campus, nestled among a cluster of pine trees off the main sidewalk, where I could sit down between classes to relax, reflect, and ponder the meaning of life. From my spot I could clearly see the Rocky Mountains and the majesty of Mount Olympus. I often spent time praying while looking at the mountains and contemplating the splendor and majesty of all our Maker had given us. As my eyes turned heavenward, so did my thoughts and heart. I decided to take my concerns to Heavenly Father in sincere prayer at my special spot, where I could be alone and pray.

It was in the fall of the year, and the leaves were just turning red, orange, and a beautiful bright yellow. The air was crisp, and the sky was a deep blue. My decision weighed heavily on my mind. Should I marry the man I was dating or not? I was aware that our relationship had reached the point where we needed to move toward marriage, or it needed to end.

I did as the scriptures teach—I studied the matter out in my mind, made a decision, and prayed. This young man seemed like the perfect choice for me. I knew the Lord loved him and that the Lord loved me, too. I knew that if it was right for us to be together, I would feel at peace inside as I prayed. I made the decision that I did want to marry him, and I took that decision to the Lord.

As I prayed, tears welled up in my eyes as I continued to feel turmoil and confusion inside, rather than the peace and contentment I wanted. The Lord's reply seemed clear, yet I was having a hard time with my feelings. I reasoned that perhaps I hadn't prayed sincerely enough or listened long enough; therefore, I asked again and again, but I felt the same confusion.

I decided to reverse my decision to see if that made a difference. As I did, I felt peace inside. That was not the answer I wanted.

Tears flowed freely as I realized how difficult it would be for me to give up my own personal desires to follow the impressions I had felt in prayer. I sat quietly and wept, not understanding why I was not supposed to marry him and feeling deeply heartbroken. I began almost begging Heavenly Father to help me feel peaceful inside about marrying him. At that moment a wonderful thing happened.

Words began to flow freely into my mind. I didn't hear an audible voice, but I clearly heard a voice—a spiritual one. I understood the words and the message. The voice said, "Trust in the Lord with all thine heart; and lean not unto thine own understanding. In all thy ways acknowledge him, and he shall direct thy paths" (Proverbs 3:5-6).

I didn't recall consciously knowing these words, but they sounded like a verse from the scriptures. I had no idea, however, where it would be found if it was there. As I sat and pondered the words "Trust in the Lord . . . lean not unto thine own understanding," I was filled with the Spirit and finally felt some peace.

I felt that the Lord knew me and knew of my yearnings. My heart felt comforted. The Lord knew me! And he knew the deepest yearnings of my heart.

I got up from my special spot and hurried off to class. The message continued to flow in my mind for several days. I felt a surge of strength and a renewed commitment to truly put my trust in the Lord. I knew, with his help, that I could do this difficult thing.

That Sunday our stake was having stake conference. We were to sustain a new patriarch, so it was our privilege to have one of the Twelve Apostles, Elder Thomas S. Monson, as a visiting General Authority. So many people were expected to attend conference that they assigned half the wards to meet at 8:30 a.m. and the other half at 11:00 a.m.

I was still struggling with the answer I had received earlier in the week. At times I felt strong, and at other times I felt very weak. I was looking forward to Sunday, hoping to be strengthened by the message Elder Monson would give to us.

I spent the morning fasting and praying to be in tune with the Spirit. Our ward was to meet at the 11:00 a.m. session. My family was usually late to conference, but that day we got there early and sat in the chapel. I was pleased that we were able to secure seats close to the front.

The low buzz of people talking filled the air as everyone anticipated hearing from one of the Lord's Apostles. As Elder Monson walked in that Sunday, he radiated warmth and love. As the conference progressed, my heart started to swell inside me. I felt warm all over. The Spirit filled my whole being. Was everyone feeling what I was feeling, or was I especially close to the Spirit because of my fast? The thought went through my mind that perhaps I would be called on to bear my testimony. What would I say? Then I thought of my experience a few days earlier of receiving an answer to my prayers. The words "Trust in the Lord" came back to me. I could share that sweet experience!

I was not called on, but when Elder Monson stood to speak,

I realized that the experience had been called back to my mind as a second witness that I had received an answer to my prayers.

Elder Monson said, "I came today with a talk I had prepared to give to you. [He had given it in the morning session.] But as I have sat here in this session, the Spirit has whispered to me to give you a different message, and so, humbly, I do. I take my text from Proverbs 3:5-6:

Trust in the Lord with all thine heart; and lean not unto thine own understanding.

In all thy ways acknowledge him, and he shall direct thy paths (Prov. 3:5-6)."

Elder Monson was unaware of the young twenty-one-year-old woman sitting back five or six rows, with her head bowed and tears flowing freely down her cheeks. I felt as though the Lord were speaking directly through him to me.

I followed that counsel by the Spirit to trust in the Lord, and I broke off the relationship with the young man I had thought I would marry. We sat in my living room and wept together. It was difficult to break up, but he seemed to feel the decision was right, too. I knew I had made the right decision because of the peace I felt.

Within a short time, this young man became engaged to someone else. I knew Heavenly Father was guiding our paths, but I still struggled, and I still felt deeply hurt. A few days after the announced engagement, my father stayed home from work to give me a blessing.

Dad said, "Diane, you have been through a lot. Do you think you have made the right decision?"

I looked at him in a daze and said, "I don't know, Dad." It seems to be human nature that even after so many witnesses, we can still doubt! At that moment I said, "Heavenly Father, help me to know if I have done what is right." As I had those thoughts, the telephone rang. It was my Uncle Evan calling from Logan, asking for me. He said, "I was sitting in my office and had the feeling I should call you. I know you have been through a lot the last few days. What you are doing is the Lord's will. He is aware of you." He went on, "You must trust him with all your heart."

I now knew without a doubt that Heavenly Father was mindful of me. Uncle Evan had no way of knowing I had been praying or what I had been praying about, except through the Spirit.

Many times circumstances we don't understand will occur in our lives. With our finite minds, we cannot see the beginning from the end. Yet God sees the big picture, and he knows what experiences we need to shape our lives.

Joseph Smith, Sr., saw his crops fail three years in a row. How discouraging that must have been! Because of that trial, he was forced to move his family to a township just outside Palmyra, New York. In retrospect, of course, we know that is where his son, Joseph Smith, Jr., needed to be to receive the golden plates from Moroni. We can't see the whole picture. Sometimes it is to our advantage that we do not know the full extent of a particular trial, so that we can learn to grow in trust and faith.

I didn't get married the next year, or the next. In fact, seven years came and went. I was twenty-eight years old when I finally got married. Heavenly Father knew that of all the experiences in this life that would humble me, one of the best would be for me to be single for many years and experience a time of yearning, of desiring and wanting something with all my heart. Some may say that being single would be an easy trial, and for some it may be easy, but for me it was a difficult challenge.

God knows what trials each person needs in order to grow. I believe we are often given the very challenge that is the most difficult for us to face.

Over the years as I have spoken to audiences at firesides and conferences, I have heard many stories that have helped me to become sensitive to others' challenges. I would like to share with you the experiences of several other people who have learned to put their trust in the Lord.

The first is a young woman named Diane Ellingson. The first

time I met Diane, I knew she was a person I wanted to get to know. She radiated warmth and peace. Her story touched my heart, as well as the hearts of thousands of other people.

In 1972, Diane watched the Olympics on television with her family. She was thrilled as she watched gymnast Olga Korbut move gracefully and flawlessly on the uneven parallel bars. She decided that she had to become a gymnast!

Diane asked her parents for the opportunity to take gymnastics lessons. They were pleased with her ambition, but finances were tight at the time; the family was supporting two brothers on missions. Another consideration was the fact that there was no gym close by, and Diane had no transportation to get to the closest one.

Her heart sank, yet the vision lived on inside her. She could see herself on the balance beam, twirling around the uneven bars, dancing gracefully on the ground, and lifting high above the horse doing flips. She thought about gymnastics and lived them constantly in her mind. She practiced on the grass in back of her house and taught herself all the gymnastic basics. Not surprisingly, it all came easily to her. It was as though her body was made to be a gymnast.

Diane also took some gymnastics classes at school. She learned as much as she could on her own without lessons. She even competed for her junior high school by teaching herself routines from books.

Two years later, when she was fourteen and in the ninth grade, the Utah Academy of Gymnastics moved into the old Sherman Elementary School just a few blocks from her home. She was very excited!

Shortly after the sign went up on the building, Diane's gym teacher, knowing that she had potential, talked to the owners and teachers of the Academy and arranged a meeting to discuss the possibility of Diane's being a janitor in exchange for lessons. The instructor agreed to give her a try, since a janitor hadn't yet been hired.

Six months later, she had been made a junior leader and was

able to help teach classes and spot younger children to pay for her gymnastics lessons.

She learned five or six new things every day. In about eight months, she had skipped all the levels and was trying to get into Olympic-level competition. She learned quickly and easily in the next few years. She began training in the afternoons and teaching at night as she continued to pay for her own training.

In high school, her life was focused on gymnastics. She finished school classes at 1:00 p.m. and spent the rest of the day— until 9:00 p.m.—training and teaching at the Academy. She loved the feeling of her body whirling freely around the bars with such ease, and the feeling of being in control of every graceful move.

Diane went on to win the Junior Olympic National Championship, which was a highlight in her gymnastics career. Then she had to decide whether to go back and try to make Elite (the highest level for gymnasts) and wait for the Olympics in three more years or to go on to college.

Greg Marsden, women's gymnastics coach at the University of Utah, offered her a full scholarship at the university. She had enjoyed teaching the small children at the Academy, so she decided to accept the scholarship and major in elementary education at the university.

During her freshman year, Diane was ranked fourth in the nation in gymnastics. She won every meet she was in all season. Just before the national competition, she injured her foot and therefore only competed on the uneven parallel bars. She won All-American.

Diane made a prediction that before she graduated the University of Utah would win the national title, and in her senior year that prediction came true. Her team won their first national title. The University of Utah Women's Gymnastics Team was #1 in the nation!

After graduation, Diane received an offer to join a pro tour going on the road with a professional gymnastics show similar to Ice Capades, with costumes and special effects. She accepted the offer and flew to Florida to start rehearsals. Two days into her professional career, her life changed dramatically forever.

Diane was trying to learn a vault called a handspring front somersault. When the coach who was spotting her ran across the gym to get something, she thought, "I'll just do some timers while I'm waiting for him."

A "timer" means that instead of pushing off the bar with your hands and doing a somersault, you push off your hands and land on your feet without doing the somersault. Diane pushed off too hard with her hands and couldn't get her feet around and down in time. Rather than landing on her feet, she landed on the back of her head.

When she landed she felt a tingly feeling shoot through her body and into her legs. Then she felt heavy; she couldn't sit up or move. The paramedics were called, and she was put on a stretcher and rushed to the hospital.

Diane was conscious and even making jokes, but she later admitted being very frightened. She knew the accident had been serious, but she hoped there would be no permanent injury. The doctors were also hopeful. A spinal cord injury can cause a person to be temporarily paralyzed, but after the inflammation goes down in a few weeks, if the spinal cord is totally intact, the person may completely recover.

On December 28, Diane was flown back to Salt Lake City in a Lear jet. She spent the next five months at the University Medical Center, with forty of those days in traction. She describes that time as the most discouraging and depressing period of her whole life. She had gone from being extremely active to being bedridden. She hit rock bottom.

It was difficult for her parents to see her suffer and be in such pain, and also to feel her deep discouragement. They came to the hospital every night, held her hand, and had family prayer. Her father gave her many blessings, and the Spirit was very comforting to her.

Elder Neal A. Maxwell also gave her a blessing while she was still in traction. When he came to see her, she told him she knew he had the power of God to heal her. She said, "I have been praying long and hard for many days. Tonight I want to make sure that whatever happens to me is what is supposed to happen."

He agreed and then gave her a beautiful blessing. He told Diane she would inspire thousands of people, and that if it was the Lord's will, she'd walk again. He also said if it wasn't the Lord's will that she walk again, there would be a greater purpose in her life.

Many years have passed. Diane is still confined to a wheelchair, yet she is completely independent. She has found a way to share her experiences and to be of service to others. She has become an excellent speaker. It is touching to watch the screen above her as she speaks and to see slides of her as a gymnast with her agile, graceful body—and then to look below the slides at the young lady sitting in a wheelchair, whose movements are now curtailed so drastically.

Nevertheless, Diane radiates a lovely spirit, and people love being with her. Diane said to me, "I think my purpose is to use my life and my experiences to lift other people—to reach out and help others who may be struggling. I have been through a lot of difficulty, but then everybody has difficult times. Perhaps I can share my experiences with others so they can be inspired when life is going differently for them than they had planned. Perhaps they can gain courage when difficulties arise.

"Looking back now, I can honestly say when I was a gymnast I gave 100 percent. I have no regrets. I know I reached my potential as a gymnast. I accomplished everything I could. My philosophy was always, 'Reach for the stars, and you might get lucky and peak the mountains.' I did reach for the stars—I wanted to go to the Olympics, and I became the Junior Olympic Champion.

"And now, today, I am still giving 100 percent. The arena has changed, but I'm giving my all. *Now I put my trust in God.* My life is in his hands. As President Ezra Taft Benson once said, ' . . . he [God] can make a lot more of our lives than we can' (*New Era,*

May 1975, p. 20). I am finding that to be true. I desire more than anything to live with the Lord again one day. That is the vision that lives on inside of me today.

"Reach for the stars, and you might get lucky and peak the mountains. I am reaching for the stars and, in the process, catching a glimpse of heaven." (This story also appeared in the book "Don't You *Dare* Give Up" by Renon Klossner Hulet, Deseret Book, 1992.)

Our lives are much like a piece of clay in the hands of a potter. The potter slaps it in his hands and puts it on the potter's wheel. He then begins to mold a beautiful vase. As he begins to shape it, he tears away at the lump on one side, pokes at it on the other side, smooths some of the rough edges, and then rips away part of it again. Over and over, he bends and cuts and shapes it until at last he has fashioned the clay into a most magnificent vase.

There is a Master Potter who is carefully shaping each of us through our experiences into what he would have us become. He knows exactly how to shape us, how to mold us, and how to get us to the point where we will put our whole trust in him as we learn to rely on the Spirit.

Every person alive has a purpose on this earth. If our purposes were fulfilled, we would be called home to be with our Maker. But our purposes are not yet fulfilled; there is more he would have us do. And for those who have lived righteously, when their purposes in this life are fulfilled, they will be called home to participate in the great and glorious work on the other side of the veil.

A few years ago, a friend of mine was killed in an automobile accident when her car rolled over on the freeway. That same weekend, a young man in our ward was in another unrelated automobile accident. His car went off a cliff, down a ravine, and rolled six times. He got up and walked away. His accident was much more serious, but his life's purpose was not yet fulfilled. Both of these people were living righteous lives. One was called home, and one was allowed to stay.

Heavenly Father sees the whole picture. He knows our hearts

and our heartaches, and he alone knows when our journey on this earth is over. While we are here, he knows the areas in each of our lives that will best test us—-areas in which we will learn to turn our hearts heavenward and to trust in him. In the scriptures we read, "For my thoughts are not your thoughts. Neither are your ways my ways" (Isaiah 55:8). The Lord has also said, "But it must needs be done in mine own way . . ." (D&C 104:16). Each of us will face trials in which we will need to turn to the Lord for help and strength.

In 1984, President Ezra Taft Benson said:

> It is in the depths where men and women learn the lessons which help them gain strength, not at the pinnacle of success. The hour of man's success is his greatest danger. It sometimes takes reverses to make us appreciate our blessings and to develop us into strong courageous characters. We can meet every reverse that can possibly come with the help of the Lord. (Conf. Report of Denmark, Finland, Norway, and Sweden Area Conference 1974, p. 70. Used by permission.)

We are God's chosen children, who were kept back in the spirit world to come forth at this time for a glorious purpose. Our Heavenly Father has a purpose for you and for me. As we pray humbly, we can find out what that purpose is and what Heavenly Father would have us do. The Lord will not leave us alone. He cares about what is happening in our lives.

Donna Frame is another person who has learned to trust in the Lord. Donna grew up in Idaho Falls, Idaho. As a young woman, she looked forward to getting married and having a large family because she loved children.

Donna married her sweetheart, Fred, but as the years went by they were unable to have children. After six years of disappointment, Donna and Fred decided to adopt a baby. While they were waiting to adopt, Donna had to have a hysterectomy. This dashed her hopes of ever bearing a child of her own.

Right after she returned home from the operation, Donna and Fred received some joyful news. The adoption agency called and told them they had a baby boy for them to adopt. This was the happiest news they could have received. They named the child Doug.

A few years later, Donna and Fred were able to adopt again—this time a baby girl, whom they named Marie. As the years passed, this little family spent many happy times together.

One rainy evening, they needed to take their car in for some repairs. They traveled from Boise, Idaho, to neighboring Nampa to a repair shop. Donna was in one car with little Marie, and Fred was in the other car with Doug.

At the intersection where they would normally turn, Donna was puzzled because Fred turned the wrong way. She decided to go ahead and make the correct turn. That decision saved Donna the agony of witnessing the accident that took her husband's life.

She said to Marie, "We'll race them and get there first." Donna was right—they got there first. They pulled their car over to wait for Fred and Doug. They waited and waited and waited, but Fred and Doug didn't show up.

Donna and Marie decided to have a prayer, after which Donna had a strong impression to call her father, who lived in Boise, and ask him if he had heard from Fred. Donna dialed the number and her father picked up the phone. The moment he heard Donna's voice he said, "Oh, Donna, where are you? We just received a phone call from the hospital. Fred has been in a terrible automobile accident . . . Donna . . . Fred has been killed. . . . Doug is still alive, but seriously hurt. We've been praying you would call. Please hurry to the hospital, and we will meet you there."

Doug was miraculously spared, but Donna now had to pick up the pieces of her life without her husband. "I have never struggled so hard as I did those next three years," she said. "My sweetheart, the person I cared about the very most in all the world, was gone. Sundays were especially hard because that is the day when families are together, and I felt like half a family, not a whole one."

After several years Donna met a man from Price, Utah, named Mick Frame, whose wife had died a few years earlier, leaving him with a family of nine children. Mick's wife had died the very same day Fred had died three years earlier.

Mick and Donna fell in love and married, and for the past eight years Donna has been raising a family of *eleven* children. The woman who could not have her own—who loved children more than anything else—has now had the opportunity to be a mother to eleven!

Throughout the scriptures, we see many accounts of the Father and Son showing compassion as people have suffered trials and tribulation. One of these was the Prophet Joseph Smith. During his moment of greatest despair in Liberty Jail, these words of total understanding and compassion came to him: ". . . Know thou my son, that all these things shall give thee experience, and shall be for thy good. The Son of Man hath descended below them all. Art thou greater than he?" (D&C 122:7-8).

Brigham Young explained that trials are necessary if we are to be perfected:

> Joseph could not have been perfected, though he had lived a thousand years, if he had received no persecution. If he had lived a thousand years and led this people and preached the gospel without persecution, he would not have been perfected as well as he was at the age of 39 years. (Brigham Young, Journal of Discourses 2:7)

All of us experience trials, tribulation, persecution, or difficulties in our lives. As we look to those who have gone before and who have been guided by the Spirit, we learn that it is in our times of trial that we grow in strength.

There is a Master Potter who is very much aware of us. We are in his hands, and he is shaping our lives. The more we learn to trust him, the greater peace we will feel in the times when he is shaping us to his purposes.

Chapter Three

TAKING THE HOLY SPIRIT FOR OUR GUIDE

Many years ago, I heard the story (told at a BYU fireside) of a young black man named Len Hope, who grew up in the South in humble circumstances. He was a God-fearing man who enjoyed studying the Bible. One day he read that in the days after Christ, on the day of Pentecost, the Spirit of God came upon the people.

He was puzzled about why he didn't feel the Spirit, and he realized it was something he desired very much. He told his mother of his desire, and of his decision to go to the hills and pray to ask God how he could receive the Holy Ghost.

Len went into the back hills a distance from his home, where he spent several days praying and thinking. He prayed, "God, the scriptures tell us that we can have the Spirit. I don't feel like I have it. I want to know how I can get the Holy Ghost." As he prayed, an impression came to him: "Go home, Len. This is not the way to get the Holy Ghost. Go home, and I will show you how." Len was filled with joy at the answer he had received.

At the same time, on a country road near his home, two Mormon missionaries walked along, feeling hot, sweaty, and uncomfortable from the moist heat. One of the elders turned to the other and said, "I have a strong feeling we should go down that lane over there." The two elders walked down the dusty road until they came to a humble home, where they felt impressed to stop. They knocked and a woman came to the door. She said, "Yes, may I help you?"

The elder said, "Hello, Ma'am. I feel impressed to ask you if you have a son."

She said, "Why, yes, but he is away for a few days."

The elder said, "Would you give him this information when he returns?" He handed her a pamphlet and said, "Tell him we will come back in a few days."

In the meantime, Len traveled home. He told his mother of his experience, and she told him about the two young men dressed in white shirts and nice slacks who had come by and left a pamphlet. She handed Len the pamphlet, which he immediately read. It was a pamphlet on the Holy Ghost—a direct answer to his prayers!

The missionaries returned, and Len was taught the gospel, baptized, and confirmed a member of the Church. He had at last received the gift of the Holy Ghost. (Complete account given in BYU fireside talk by Max Pinegar, September 28, 1975.)

Since then, Len has married a member of the Church and is raising a righteous family. How very blessed he is, and those like him who have the wonderful gift of the Holy Ghost. That gift is available to *all* who will receive it.

In speaking of the Holy Ghost, Parley P. Pratt said:

> An intelligent being in the image of God possesses every organ, attribute, sense, sympathy, affection of will, wisdom, love, power and gift which is possessed by God himself. But these attributes are in embryo and are to be gradually developed. *The Gift of the Holy Spirit adapts itself to all of these organs or attributes. It quickens all the intellectual faculties and increases, enlarges, expands and purifies all the natural passions and affections and adapts them by the gift of wisdom to their lawful use. It inspires, develops, cultivates, and matures all the fine tone sympathies, joys, tastes, kindred feelings and affections of our nature. It inspires virtue, kindness, goodness, tenderness, gentleness and charity. It develops beauty of person, form, and features. It tends to health, vigor, animation, and social feelings. It develops and invigorates all the fac-*

ulties of the physical and intellectual man.
(Quoted by James E. Talmage in *A Study of the Articles of Faith* [Salt Lake City: Church of Jesus Christ of Latter-day Saints, 1964], p. 487. Italics added. Used by permission.)

From the parable of the ten virgins in Matthew 25:1-13, we learn that at the Savior's second coming, only those with oil in their lamps will be prepared to meet him. As a child, I was worried about this parable. It upset me that the virgins wouldn't share their oil. I visualized them carrying large camp lanterns. As I matured, I learned that the Savior was referring to a small lamp shaped like a pear that fits snugly in the palm of the hand. On the wide end of the lamp is a hole about an inch in diameter, which serves as a reservoir for the oil. At the other, smaller end is a tiny hole about the diameter of a pencil, from which the wick extends to hold the flame.

Another false idea I had as a child was that the five wise virgins represented the members of the Church at the Second Coming, and the five foolish virgins represented those who had never been baptized. I now know that this parable refers only to members of the Church—those who have received the truth and been baptized.

It seems imperative that we learn to understand the analogy of the oil and the lamps in order to be prepared for the Second Coming. What is it that we need in order to be among the half who are wise and prepared?

The seeming selfishness of the virgins confused me until I came to understand the full meaning of the parable and what the oil stands for. The Savior gave us the answer in Doctrine and Covenants 45:56-57:

And at that day, when I shall come in my glory, shall the parable be fulfilled which I spake concerning the ten virgins.

For they that are wise and have received the truth, *and have taken the Holy Spirit for their guide,* and have not been deceived—therefore I say unto you, they shall not be hewn down and cast into the fire, but shall abide the day (Italics added).

The key words in this scripture are those in italics: "and have taken the Holy Spirit for their guide." The Holy Ghost is the light or lamp that guides our lives. It is not possible for us to share our oil, which is the price we have paid to have the companionship of the Holy Ghost. The oil is everything we do in our lives that helps us to have the Holy Ghost as our guide. Each time we pray, read the scriptures, fast, think loving thoughts, or humble ourselves before the Lord, we add oil to our lamps. We can tell we are being guided by the Holy Ghost every time we live a commandment, every time we go to the temple, and every time we show love, concern, and understanding for others.

On the other hand, when we give in to worldly enticements, such as going to R-rated movies, casinos, or any other unholy place where the Spirit cannot dwell, we are figuratively turning our lamps upside down and dumping out the oil. When we say or do unkind things to our husbands or wives or yell at our children, the oil starts draining. When we turn on loud music that alienates the Spirit, participate in vulgarity, or take harmful things into our bodies, we are emptying oil from our lamps.

Concerning the parable of the ten virgins, Elder Wilford Woodruff declared:

The parable of ten virgins is intended to represent the second coming of the Son of man, the coming of the bridegroom to meet the bride, the Church, the Lamb's wife, in the last day; and I expect the Savior was about right when he said, in reference to the members of the Church, that five of them were wise and five were foolish; for when the Lord of Heaven comes in power and great glory to reward every man according to the deeds done in the body, if he finds one half of those professing to be members of his Church prepared for salvation, it will be as many as can be expected, judging by the course that many are pursuing. (Journal of Discourses 18:110)

We all experience trials, frustrations, and problems. We can get caught up in the concerns of day-to-day living, health problems, financial pressures, problems with a spouse or a child, and pressures at work. Frustrations might even be caused by something as simple as car problems, losing something, or difficulty with some household task. Whatever the cause, all of us experience moments of frustration and daily concerns that try our patience and, at times, our faith. As these concerns arise, how do we cope with them? Do we rely on the Spirit to help us?

There are two positive ways to handle problems, concerns, and frustrations. These two ways go hand in hand. First, we must strive to live as righteously as we can. Second, we must exercise faith by praying earnestly, listening for the promptings of the Holy Ghost, and following the promptings we receive.

Learning to follow these promptings is a lifelong pursuit for most of us.

Generally, we don't act on knowledge; we act on how we feel. That is why it is so important to feel the Spirit, for the Spirit—the Holy Ghost—speaks the words of Christ, and the words of Christ will tell us all things that we should do.

Let's explore some of the ways the Spirit communicates to us.

The Spirit Speaks Peace to Our Hearts

One way the Spirit communicates with us is by blessing us with a peaceful feeling in our hearts. When he was serving as a scribe while Joseph Smith translated the Book of Mormon, Oliver

Cowdery also desired to be able to translate. In response to that desire came a message to him from the Lord:

> Verily, verily, I say unto you, if you desire a further witness, cast your mind upon the night that you cried unto me in your heart, that you might know concerning the truth of these things.
>
> Did I not speak peace to your mind concerning the matter? What greater witness can you have than from God? (D&C 6:22-23)

At the age of twenty-six, I entered the Missionary Training Center in Provo, Utah. I loved the Lord dearly, but I struggled with the feeling that I really didn't want to be on a mission—at least not at twenty-six. I wanted to be married and having children. Satan was working hard on me. I had struggled with the decision to serve a mission, but undeniable impressions to go had come to me. Now, I continued to struggle.

One night as I lay on my bed, I could feel opposition all around me. I felt as if I was going to be destroyed. It was the most frightening feeling I have ever had in my life. I finally crawled out of bed onto my knees and pleaded for help. As I prayed, the darkness vanished. A beautiful light filled my mind, and I experienced a most peaceful feeling. A few weeks later, as I arrived in the mission field in the Belgium Brussels Mission, our mission president interviewed each new missionary personally.

When I finished my interview, the mission president said he would like to offer a special prayer in my behalf, as he did with each missionary. He asked if there were any special blessings I needed. "Nothing that I can think of," I replied. As he began the prayer, my MTC experience came back to my mind. I realized that I did desire a blessing that I would be protected from Satan. I also wished I had talked to the president about my concern about finding someone to marry when I returned from my mission. But his prayer had already begun.

I silently resolved that when I got home that night, I would pour out my heart in fervent prayer, asking Heavenly Father for help with those two things.

No sooner had those thoughts gone through my mind than President Hatch said in his prayer, "Diane, I bless you that Satan shall have absolutely no power over you on this mission. And I bless you also that the Lord will preserve a young man for you to marry, who will be there for you when you get home from your mission." The Spirit had communicated my needs and desires to my mission president, with no need for words from me! Once again I experienced a feeling of great peace. As the scriptures say, "What greater witness can you have than from God?" (D&C 6:23).

When we feel peaceful and content about something, it is usually the Holy Ghost letting us know it is good or right. Imparting a sweet feeling of peace to our hearts is one distinctive way the Holy Ghost communicates with us.

A Burning in the Bosom

Another way the Spirit communicates to us is through a burning in the bosom. These verses from the Doctrine and Covenants describe that phenomenon:

> But, behold, I say unto you, that you must study it out in your mind; then you must ask me if it be right, and if it is right I will cause that your bosom shall burn within you; therefore, you shall feel that it is right. But if it be not right you shall have no such feelings, but you shall have a stupor of thought that shall cause you to forget the thing which is wrong. . . . (D&C 9:8-9)

While on my mission, at times I felt overwhelmed with learning the French language. I had hated French in junior high school; now, many years later, I found myself in a French-speaking mission trying to learn it again! In the Missionary Training Center, I had learned the language well enough to converse with the other missionaries in French. However, there is a big difference between Americans speaking French and French people speaking French!

I had been out in the mission field for a few months, having just passed off all my discussions, when I learned that I would be made a senior companion at my next transfer. Fear filled my heart. I was shocked that the mission president wanted me to be a senior companion. I hoped with all my heart that my junior companion would know the language well, because I had not mastered it yet. I could engage in simple conversations and rattle off the discussions, but I didn't feel comfortable enough with the language to carry on an intelligent conversation.

Then word came from mission headquarters that I would be training a *new* missionary who was just arriving in Europe! It was an overwhelming blow.

My own senior companion had been a tremendous strength to me when I was a new missionary. She was in the last months of her mission and spoke fluent French. I had leaned heavily on her in those early weeks because of her ability to communicate with the people so well. But for me to have to train a brand-new missionary was almost more than I could comprehend. I knew in my heart I could not be the same strength to my new companion that my first companion had been to me.

I felt terribly upset that day. Feelings of inadequacy and anxiety filled my heart. My senior companion was preparing to go home the next day. She tried to console me, embracing me and saying, "Don't worry, Diane, things will work out. You'll do just fine."

We had been tracting and teaching all morning, and had come home for our noon meal. I knew I needed help from Heavenly Father, so I went into the bathroom while my companion was in the kitchen preparing lunch. I told her to go ahead with her lunch because I needed to pray.

I told Heavenly Father how inadequate I felt. I told him I

didn't feel ready to be a senior companion to a brand-new missionary. I shared all my doubts and feelings. As I prayed, I felt a beautiful sweet peace. A warmth began to glow and burn inside me, and then swelled and expanded until it filled my entire being. I knew . . . I knew that everything *would* be okay.

I didn't know what was going to happen in the next few days. Maybe I would suddenly be given the gift of tongues and be able to speak French with ease. Maybe my new companion would be a sister who had taken French all through high school and college. Whatever the circumstances, I knew in my heart that everything would be all right.

I had been in our little bathroom for a good portion of our lunch break, but I came out with a big smile on my face. Sister Goepp took one look at me and said, "Something's happened to you."

I assured her, "Everything *is* going to be okay. I don't know how, but everything's going to be okay." The fear in my heart had totally evaporated, and now my heart was filled with faith.

The next day I bid farewell to my companion, and the elders took me to the train station to pick up my new companion. As we stood there anxiously looking around, I wondered if this new sister would be as frightened as I was when I arrived in my new area all by myself and was unable to communicate with the people.

Then I saw her! She looked like a brand-new missionary— totally lost! She looked around as if she didn't know where to go or what to do. She was loaded down with luggage, bags, books, and a camera.

I couldn't let her wait a minute longer. I ran to her, threw my arms around her, and said, "Welcome to Europe!" She looked at me somewhat puzzled, and then, after an embarrassing pause, she said, "Je ne parle pas Anglaise." Interpreted, that means, "I don't speak English."

Then I threw my arms around her again and gave her an even tighter hug. She was still puzzled, but I wasn't. Heavenly Father had sent me a new companion who spoke *only* French! What a glorious blessing that was for me. Before our companionship ended, Sister Billeri had mastered the discussions, and I finally felt comfortable with the language.

Pure Intelligence

Another way the Spirit communicates with us is through pure intelligence. Thoughts can come into our minds and assist us in understanding something completely or in becoming aware of something we should know. The scriptures describe it this way: "Yea, behold, I will tell you in your mind and in your heart, by the Holy Ghost, which shall come upon you and which shall dwell in your heart" (D&C 8:2).

One day I was busily working in my kitchen. I suddenly had the forceful feeling that I should check on my tiny daughter. I didn't hear words, but I had an overwhelming *knowingness* that it was important to check on my crawling infant. She was sitting by one of the closets sucking on something.

I immediately stuck my finger into my baby's mouth and pulled out a tiny nail about half an inch long. It was a size the baby could have swallowed easily. Had she done so, it could have done great damage to her internal organs. I humbly thanked Heavenly Father for making me aware of the danger.

Another example of this principle occurred one particular night when I felt the need to be at the temple. I love going to the temple; it's my favorite place. That night, I had taken care of everything at home with the children and was on my way to the temple.

Almost halfway there, I suddenly had an overwhelming feeling that I should go home. I drove on, but as I got closer, I had the feeling again.

I thought, "No, I'm almost to the temple." But the feeling persisted, and I finally turned my car around and headed for home, somewhat discouraged. It was dusk—just dark enough that cars have a difficult time seeing things outside clearly. As I turned my car onto the busy street where we lived, I saw my three-year-old daughter out in the street. I stopped my car, hopped out, and gathered her up in my arms.

What might have happened to my precious daughter had I not responded to those promptings? I was so grateful that night for the impressions of the Spirit.

The Spoken Word

Another way we learn from the Spirit is through words either spoken out loud, so the sound can be heard by our ears, or to our minds and our hearts.

A woman I know related an experience when she was at a point of total despair. She felt she could not handle her trials any longer. She fell prostrate on the ground and cried out to God in prayer, pleading with him and begging him to help.

As she cried out, these words were spoken to her mind: "Fear not, I am with thee; oh, be not dismayed, for I am thy God and will still give thee aid. I'll strengthen thee, help thee, and cause thee to stand, upheld by my righteous omnipotent hand." (*Hymns of The Church of Jesus Christ of Latter-day Saints*, No. 85. Salt Lake City: The Church of Jesus Christ of Latter-day Saints, 1985.)

Those words were spoken to her not in an audible voice, but in a spiritual voice that came to her mind, giving her great comfort.

The Spirit Tastes Sweet

The Prophet Joseph Smith described another way the Spirit communicates to us:

This is good doctrine. It tastes good. I can taste the principles of eternal life and so can you. They are given to me by the revelations of Jesus Christ and I know when I tell you these words of eternal life, as they were given to me, you taste them. And I know that you believe them. You say honey is sweet and so do I. I can also taste the spirit of eternal life. I know it is good and when I tell you of these things which were given me by the inspiration of the Holy Spirit you are bound to receive them as sweet and rejoice more and more.

And as I read that I thought of the imagery of the tree of life and how they tasted the fruit. It was sweet and it was sweet unto them." (*Teachings of the Prophet Joseph Smith*. Salt Lake City: Deseret Book Company, 1979, p. 355.)

Dreams, Visions, and Visitations

In addition to the ways we have discussed, the Holy Ghost also communicates to us through dreams, visions, and visitations. You may be familiar with the dreams of Lehi, Nebuchadnezzar, Joseph of Egypt, and others. For example, the wisemen who followed the star when Jesus was born were "warned of God in a dream that they should not return to Herod, [and] they departed into their own country another way" (Matt. 2:12). And in the Book of Mormon, we read that "the Lord warned Omer in a dream that he should depart out of the land" (Ether 9: 3).

A more recent example is the true story of Marie Madalaine, who grew up in the Piedmont region of northern Italy. She was one of the Waldesians, a God-fearing people who had been persecuted for centuries.

At the age of six or seven, Marie was lying on her bed one day when an unusual feeling came over her. She recalled, "I saw before me, myself as a young woman, sitting on a little strip of land out on my father's pasture. As I was sitting there, some men came up to me. I was startled but they said, 'Fear not. For we bring you the restored gospel of Jesus Christ.' Then they took some little books out of their pocket and said, 'Read these and you will learn for yourself.' Then the vision closed."

Young Marie came down the stairs, walked into the kitchen, and said, "Mother, I need to talk to you."

Her mother looked at her, saw that she was pale, and said, "Marie, is something wrong?" Marie began to explain, but her mother interrupted and said, "Sit right here on this bench while I attend to some things and I will be with you in a moment."

Her father walked into the room at that moment, and Marie's mother told him something had happened to Marie. Her father asked her what had happened.

Marie related the vision to her father. She told him about the men, the book, and what they had said about the gospel. He listened intently, saying little, but tucking the information into his heart.

One day several years later, her father came into the house and asked his wife, "Would you please prepare my Sunday best clothes? I am going to Palais de la Tour. Some people there are preaching of a restored gospel, and I want to know about it."

Marie and her mother gathered together the clothes, and her father left to walk the three-day distance to the neighboring town, arriving just in time to hear a man named Lorenzo Snow speak of this restored gospel.

As Marie's father listened, his heart was filled with joy. Afterwards, he went to some of the men who were teaching with Elder Snow and said, "Would you come back with me to my village to teach the people there? You can stay at my home."

They said, "Of course. We will come."

They walked the three-day journey back to the village. When they arrived and learned that the family had a daughter, they asked to meet her.

Her mother said, "Oh, Marie is out in the pasture." The three men walked out to the pasture and saw her sitting on a strip of grass. She was by now a mature young woman, about seventeen years old. They walked up to her and startled her. She looked up and they said, "Oh, do not be afraid. We have come to bring you the restored gospel of Jesus Christ." Then they reached into their pockets and pulled out little booklets, which they handed to her, saying, "Read these, and you will know for yourself."

Her vision was fulfilled to the very word. All of the family and most of the village were converted to the gospel, and traveled the long distance to America. Many later traveled across the plains with handcarts.

Marie is an example of one who had the privilege of seeing a vision. Some have received the rare blessing of a heavenly visitation, which might occur when there is a certain need. One of the most glorious of all was the visitation of God the Father and His Son, Jesus Christ to the young Joseph Smith.

Wilford Woodruff related a visitation Brigham Young received.

> One morning while we were at Winter Quarters, Brother Brigham Young said to me and the brethren that he had had a visitation the night previous from Joseph Smith. I asked him what he said to him. He replied that Joseph had told him to t*ell the people to labor to obtain the Spirit of God.* That they need it to sustain them and to give them the power to go through their work on the earth. (Wilford Woodruff, "The Necessity of Having the Holy Ghost," pamphlet copied from the *Deseret Weekly News,* vol. 53, no. 21, November 7, 1896, p. 6. Italics added for emphasis. Used by permission.)

Recognizing and Following Promptings

Have you ever had an impression and wondered, "Was that my own thinking, or was that a prompting from the Spirit?" Sometimes we brush off impressions that come. At times I have brushed impressions off as my own thoughts, only to learn later that they were impressions with consequences.

A few years ago I was scheduled to speak at a singles fireside on a Wednesday evening. That day everything went wrong. One of our cars broke down, and I wondered if I would make it to my speaking engagement. The irony is, when everything goes wrong and the opposition I am facing is extreme, I know I am definitely *supposed* to do what I am attempting to do.

Chris and I took the car in to be repaired, and we got home at about 4:30 in the afternoon.

Chris took our children to his mother's house, and I went inside to begin getting ready for my speaking engagement. Then I did something I never do. I unplugged every phone in our home. I have a difficult time not answering the phone, and I needed some peace and quiet in order to collect my thoughts before going to speak.

Many times while I am preparing to go places, I turn on the radio and listen to soft music, but that evening I even made sure the radio and television were off while I was getting dressed.

I enjoyed a spiritual evening as I spoke to some choice sons and daughters of our Father in Heaven. As soon as the fireside was over, I left to go to a choral group singing practice. I was filled with the Spirit and didn't want to disrupt the feeling. However, members were only permitted to miss a few practices, and I had missed enough that missing one more would put me in jeopardy, so I needed to make a showing.

I got in my car to go to the practice at Skyline High School, twenty minutes away. As I got in my car, an impression came: "Go home." I thought, "I can't go home. I've got to go to the practice, or I'll be kicked out of the group." I headed straight to the high school. As I drove I wondered, "Was that me, or did I have an impression?"

Arriving at the high school, I quickly got out and ran to the door. As I walked inside, it was dead silent. I walked toward the choral room and was surprised to see the doors closed. They were always open on rehearsal night.

I tried the first set of double doors, and they were locked. I shook them a little. "This is really strange," I thought. I went to the other side and did the same thing. "How weird. Where are they?" I wondered. I looked up at the wall to see if there was a note that said *Practice Has Been Canceled.*

Then it occurred to me, "Of course, they are practicing at a ward house near the University of Utah (our alternate rehearsal place). They tried to call me, but because I had unplugged all my phones, I must have missed the message."

I hurried out to my car to try to get to the other rehearsal place before they were through, but it was another twenty minutes away. As I got in my car, the thought passed through my mind: "I was here, they weren't—they can't kick me out. I think I'll go home." The impression came again: "Go home."

As I drove out of the school parking lot, I thought how I would enjoy seeing my parents, who lived just a short distance from the high school. I had been so busy that I hadn't seen them for a couple of weeks. I decided to drop in and say hello.

Just as I was turning to go to their home, the message came a third time: "Go home." This time I thought, "I'd better go home!" So I turned the opposite way and got on the freeway to go home.

I am embarrassed to admit this, but as I turned off the exit by my home, I was tempted again to ignore the prompting I had felt. I spotted the grocery store out of the corner of my eye and thought, "I could get a lot of grocery shopping done tonight because I don't have the kids. It would be really easy."

At that moment, I received the message once again—and this time very forcefully: "*Go home.*" I said to myself, "I don't think that was my own thoughts. I think I'd better go straight home."

The moment I walked inside my home, I knew something was wrong. Chris was standing, talking on the phone. Tears were streaming down his face. He said, "Diane, come on in. I think you'd better have a seat. I have some really sad news to give to you tonight."

He proceeded to tell me that my sister's husband, Bruce, had been killed that afternoon. Bruce was like a brother to me; he had been in our family for nearly twenty years. I was devastated for my sister.

Bruce had been shot by an assailant that afternoon at 4:30,

about the time I had returned home from picking up the car. My family had been trying to call me ever since he had died, but they couldn't get through because I had unplugged all the phones.

Looking back on this experience, I believe Heavenly Father wanted me to speak that night at the singles fireside, and he knew that I would not be able to speak if I received the news of Bruce's death before I left.

Bruce's death was the top news story of the day in Salt Lake City. It had been on every radio and television station throughout the evening, but my radio and television had been off that afternoon, and I hadn't turned on the car radio while I was driving to the fireside. It was as though I had been shielded from everything that had happened until *after* the fireside. As soon as I had finished speaking and had gone to my car, the Spirit gave me the message to go home. And it didn't let up until I listened to it.

Several days later, when I contacted my singing group, I found out, to my amazement, that they *had been* at the high school that night. They were surprised that I hadn't seen or heard them. One member said, "Diane, we were in the choral room. We were singing at full pitch, and we had the door wide open."

Following Our Feelings

Joseph Smith taught that we should listen to the first intimations of the Spirit:

A person may profit by noticing the first intimation of the Spirit of revelation. For instance, when you feel pure intelligence flowing into you it will give you sudden strokes of ideas so that by noticing it you may find it fulfilled that same day or soon. Those things that were presented unto your mind by the Spirit of God will come to pass. And thus by learning the Spirit of God and understanding it you may grow into the principal of revelation until you become perfect in Christ

Jesus. (*Teachings of the Prophet Joseph Smith.* Salt Lake
City: Deseret Book Company, 1979, p. 355.)

A number of years ago, I was serving in a Relief Society presidency. Our president was out of town, and before she left, she
asked us as counselors to be aware of the needs of the sisters in the
ward.

We had heard of nothing all week until we arrived at the
bishop's office on Sunday. To my dismay, we learned that an older
couple in our ward had been in an automobile accident on
Monday, and I knew that no one from the Relief Society presidency had been over to visit this dear sister.

Usually we knew about things immediately, but because the
president had been gone, we hadn't heard about it. However, I was
happy to hear that Sister Smith had only sustained a broken arm.
The Spirit whispered to me, "Diane, go see her today." I determined that as soon as church was over, I would go see Sister Smith
at her home.

With two preschoolers to juggle, by the time church was over
I was ready for a rest, but I still needed to feed my family and put
the children down for naps. It had snowed all through the night,
and all day long. We had a struggle making it home from church.
In all honesty, the last thing I wanted to do that afternoon was to
go back out in the snow.

I decided to call Sister Smith to see if she was up to a visit. We
talked and talked and had a delightful visit. Then I said, "Sister
Smith, I would really like to come and see you. Would you like a
visit?"

"I would love it," she said. "Would you come and see me?"

I said, "Yes." And then I said, "Would it be okay if I come
. . . tomorrow?"

"Please do," she said. "Come around back and knock real hard
so I can hear you. Bring your little kiddies with you, too." I hung
up the phone and took a nap.

Later that day Kenna, the Relief Society president, arrived

home and called to see how Sister Smith was. I told her what had happened and that I was going the next day to visit Winona. She said she would like to go with me and would call me first thing in the morning to set up a time.

The next morning, as expected, Kenna called me. But the moment she spoke, I could tell by the tone in her voice that something was wrong. She said, "Oh, Diane, Sister Winona Smith died last night. . . ."

I can hardly express how sorrowful I felt that I had not followed my first impressions to visit Winona that Sunday. Heavenly Father had known and had tried to tell me. I had missed an opportunity to let Sister Smith know I loved her.

Most of us have opportunities to learn firsthand the importance of following those first impressions. Our first impressions often direct us to what the Spirit would have us do.

About six years ago, I woke up one Sunday morning. The Spirit said, "Go see Grandma West today." Grandma West was Chris's grandmother. She had had Alzheimer's disease for many years. She didn't recognize me or Chris, but we visited her as often as we could at the rest home.

That Sunday morning I said, "Chris, we need to go see Grandma today. I feel it strongly."

He said, "Yes, we do need to go see her."

However, that particular Sunday my family had planned to get together for dinner. Most of my family live in Salt Lake City, but our lives are busy with Church callings, and our Sunday dinners together are infrequent. We had a dilemma on our hands.

Chris said, "We really need to get together with your family. Why don't we go see Grandma tomorrow? We can spend the whole afternoon with her, and maybe have a family home afternoon before she goes to bed around five."

I was content with that and said, "That will be fine."

That night as we arrived home and were getting ready for bed, the telephone rang. It was Chris's mother. She said, "Oh, sweethearts, Grandma West died this afternoon."

Tears came to Chris's eyes. Had we followed the promptings of the Spirit that day, we would have been in her room at the moment she passed from this life to the next. Perhaps she would have known us and would have known we cared.

Years later a dear cousin, Suzanne, had a similar strong impression to visit our Grandma Barnes, and she listened to the promptings. Suzanne's mother and father had died when she was a child. Grandma Barnes had raised their family, and she was like Suzanne's second mother. When the feelings came persistently to be at Grandma's side, Suzanne called work, rearranged her schedule, and traveled to Grandma's house. During that visit, while she was holding Grandma in her arms, this lovely woman quietly passed away. May we all follow Suzanne's example when we feel promptings from the Spirit.

Chapter Four

REACHING HEAVENWARD

During college, I had a good friend by the name of Ed Engh. As a child, Ed was active, energetic, and vibrant. At about the age of eleven, he became ill. His parents took him to see the doctor, and to their dismay, the diagnosis was a rare form of polio. Over a period of time this disease became more and more debilitating, and eventually he was confined to a wheelchair.

But Ed had a great deal of faith. Even though he couldn't go out and play ball, run, jump, and wrestle the way other boys his age did, Ed realized that he could actively use his mind. He began to study every book he could find, borrow, or buy. Many of the books he read were Church books. Ed had read most of the books on the bookshelves in his bedroom, which covered an entire wall from floor to ceiling.

When Ed was in high school, some of the popular boys befriended him and made him a part of their group. Brian, a tall, athletic boy, took a special liking to him. When Ed's name was announced at seminary graduation, Brian met Ed at the podium, picked him up out of his wheelchair, and held him up so everyone could see him. There were many moist eyes as the audience witnessed this act of love.

More than anything else, Ed wanted to go on a mission. He had been preparing for many years. He knew the scriptures, and he had studied Church history, the words of the prophets, and the doctrines of the Church. He was well grounded in the gospel.

However, Ed had been told he would not be able to go on a mission. He had visited the home of Elder Thomas S. Monson, whose daughter served on the seminary council with him.

Knowing that Elder Monson was on the Missionary Committee, Ed had asked him about the possibility of his serving a mission. Elder Monson stated that Ed's disabilities would make it difficult for him to live away from home, but he comforted Ed by suggesting that he might consider serving a stake mission.

One by one, Ed's friends received their mission calls. Brian was called to the Canada Vancouver Mission. Ed's friends promised to write, hoping he could share their missions. Yet Ed still desired with all his heart to serve a full-time mission.

I became acquainted with Ed when he and I sang in the Institute of Religion Concert Choir. He was an inspiration to everyone in the choir. Anyone who knew him was lifted by his spirit.

Ed did become a stake missionary, and he enjoyed going out with the other stake missionaries. But it still wasn't the full-time service he had hoped for.

After several months, his friend Brian was assigned to work in the mission office in Vancouver. Brian wrote to Ed, expressing his disappointment at having to spend most of the day at a typewriter in the mission office rather than finding and teaching people. Ed read that letter, and then wrote to Brian: "Be grateful you are able to serve in the mission office at a typewriter. I would give anything to be a full-time missionary for the Lord, even if it meant sitting at a typewriter for two years."

Brian was touched by the letter and took it to his mission president. As President Scott read the letter, he too was deeply moved.

President Scott then had an experience he later shared with me. He said that after reading the letter, he went into his office, where he knelt in prayer. He poured his heart out in behalf of this young man who was confined to a wheelchair. While he was praying, the quiet whisperings of the Spirit came to him with a clear answer, and he knew immediately what he should do.

He said to Brian, "Elder, I feel that Ed Engh is supposed to be a part of our mission." He asked Brian if he knew how to handle

Ed's physical needs.

Brian said, "You bet. He's one of my best friends."

President Scott called the Missionary Committee at the Church Office Building and told them there was a young man living in Salt Lake City with a physical handicap from polio, who desired to be a missionary in full-time service to the Lord. He explained that one of Ed's best friends was serving in the office and asked for permission to call him to that mission to be a companion to his friend, who knew how to take care of his physical needs. He shared with them the time he had spent in prayer, and indicated that he now felt impressed to ask that Ed be called as one of his missionaries. Before long, President Scott received word back from the Missionary Committee that his request had been granted.

Ed said, "I will never forget the day I received a phone call from Elder Monson, when he told me the Lord had prepared a way for me to go into the mission field and officially called me to serve in the Canada Vancouver Mission."

Ed had a packed house at his missionary farewell. A loving mission president and many missionaries anticipated his arrival, treated him with kindness when he arrived, and served him in many ways. He became a tremendous asset to the mission staff, and taught many people the gospel.

After Ed had been in the mission field for a few months, Elder Monson received a letter from President Scott. The president reported that Elder Engh had become a legend in their mission by establishing a standard of faith and dedication. He mentioned that Ed was serving as mission recorder. He had passed off his discussions in record time, and he and his companion had were leading their district in teaching. Mission work seemed to agree with Ed, and his health was good. President Scott and the other missionaries watched him carefully to make sure he got enough rest and a proper diet, but he did not require any extra attention.

President Scott explained that one of the reasons Elder Engh was successful was the attitude of Brian, his friend and companion. "These two elders truly have a Christlike love for one another," he said. He related a story that illustrated his point: "When Elder Engh first arrived, he expressed some concern for one of the themes of the mission, 'Lengthen Your Stride.' Elder Engh said to his companion, 'How can I lengthen my stride? I can't even walk.' Brian responded, 'That's okay, Elder, we'll just have to get you some bigger wheels.'" (Thomas S. Monson, *Be Your Best Self.* Salt Lake City: Deseret Book Company, 1979, pp. 164-165.)

Ed didn't complain about anything. He had prayed to be called on a mission, and his prayers had been answered. He didn't want to do anything that might disappoint the Lord.

Another packed house greeted Elder Engh at his missionary homecoming. Tears of joy streamed down his face. The desire of his heart had been fulfilled, and his faith had been rewarded.

Many accounts in the scriptures teach us about the blessings we can gain from exercising faith in calling down the powers of heaven in our lives. They also contain wonderful examples of people who exercised obedience and faith when it would have been easier to do otherwise. Nephi was asked to go and do a difficult task that his brothers had refused. But Nephi said,

> I will go and do the things which the Lord hath commanded, for I know that the Lord giveth no commandments unto the children of men, save he shall prepare a way for them that they may accomplish the thing which he commandeth them.
>
> And it came to pass that when my father had heard these words he was exceeding glad, for he knew that I had been blessed of the Lord. (1 Ne. 3:7-8)

Because Nephi was willing to go back to Jerusalem to obtain the brass plates, he helped to save an entire nation from ignorance regarding the commandments of God.

Jesus Christ was asked by his Father to do an even more difficult task—a task so difficult that there was no other capable of doing it. It was to be the most difficult task ever performed in the universe:

> And he went forward a little and fell on the ground, and prayed that, if it were possible, the hour might pass from him.
>
> And he said, Abba, Father, all things are possible unto thee; take away this cup from me: nevertheless not what I will, but what thou wilt. (Mark 14:35-36)

Because of his willingness to do his Father's will, the Savior was able to carry out his Father's plan to save all of God's creations.

Another young man, in a different place and time, performed another task. Feeling confused about which church to join, he pondered these words in his heart: "If any of you lack wisdom, let him ask of God that giveth to all men liberally, and upbraideth not and it shall be given him. But let him ask in faith, nothing wavering..." (James 1:5-6).

Joseph Smith went to a sacred grove of trees and there knelt in prayer. As he prayed, his fear dissipated as his faith became knowledge. Because of his obedience and faith, Joseph fulfilled his charge to bring forth the restored gospel.

So it is in our lives. God wants to bless and guide us. He will and can do so in many ways if we choose to live his commandments and draw close to him. As we draw close to him, we are empowered to draw on the powers of heaven for help in our daily lives. We read in D&C 121:36 that the powers of heaven are controlled by righteousness, and D&C 82:10 tells us that "I, the Lord, am bound when ye do what I say; but when ye do not what I say, ye have no promise."

With God's help, we can bear our daily burdens and receive great blessings. When we live as righteously as we can by being obedient to God's commandments, we can call down the powers of heaven to bless our efforts.

President Ezra Taft Benson explained how God blesses those who are sincerely trying to serve him:

> Men and women who turn their lives over to God will find out that he can make a lot more out of their lives than they can. He will deepen their joys, expand their vision, quicken their minds, strengthen their muscles, lift their spirits, multiply their blessing, increase their opportunities, comfort their souls, raise up friends and pour out peace. Whosoever will lose his life to God will find he has eternal life. (*The New Era,* May 1975, p. 20. Used by permission.)

The Powers of Heaven Can Magnify Our Intellectual Abilities

When I was a senior in high school, I took a chemistry class that was quite difficult for me. One night my friend Kim and I had a huge chemistry assignment. We hurried home from school to my house to start working on the assignment because we had a Young Women meeting that night and wanted to be through with our homework in time to attend.

When we began to work on the assignment, it didn't make any sense to us. We struggled over it. We tried to figure it out, but it seemed to be nothing but a jumble of formulas.

We became more and more frustrated as the hours passed. The time was approaching for us to leave for our meeting. We had worked most of the afternoon, with no luck in figuring out how to complete the assignment.

When it came time to leave, we were perplexed about what to do. We knew we wouldn't get home until at least 9:00 p.m. The assignment was due the next day, and we hadn't even figured out how to do it! We decided to stay home so we could get the assignment done.

However, as soon as we made that decision, we felt uneasy. It definitely didn't feel right. I felt we should go to our Young Women activity, and Kim felt the same way.

We knelt by my bed and asked Heavenly Father if he would please help us with the assignment when we returned home. We felt he wanted us to go to our activity.

When we returned at about nine, we were still faced with that horrible assignment. Once again, we got on our knees by my bed and asked Heavenly Father if he would help us.

After our prayer, I looked down at the pages in my chemistry book. My mind was opened, and the assignment began to make sense. I said, "Kim, I understand this page!"

She was looking at her book and having a similar experience. We began writing as quickly as we could, and we soon had the assignment completed. Our intellects had been enlightened. God had made known to us what we had not understood earlier, and I learned that the powers of heaven *can* magnify intellectual abilities.

During my college years, I dated a young man who made it a point never to study on the Sabbath. If he had lots of homework and hadn't completed it before the Sabbath, he would go to bed early Sunday night and arise early Monday morning to work on it. I saw how he was blessed with some academic miracles during those years, and I felt it was because he was striving to make righteous choices.

The Powers of Heaven Can Raise Up Friends

When I was in high school, I had a wonderful experience related to finding friends. I had decided to change my group of friends because my interests varied from theirs, but I soon discovered that breaking away from one group of friends and finding new friends is not easy. I found myself in no group at all.

During that time I would come home from school, throw

myself on my bed, and cry. There were days I didn't have anybody to eat lunch with at school. Even though young people were all around me, I felt alone.

I decided to pray for help. I knew God could help me, but I also knew I needed to do my part. I discovered a book on my parents' bookshelf about developing personality, and I read everything it had to say about making friends.

The book taught some valuable human relations skills. First, I learned that when you walk down the hall at school, it's important to acknowledge as many people as you can. Recognize your classmates, whether they know you or not. The first time I said hello to people I normally ignored, they looked at me as if to say, "Do I know you?" The next time, they responded and said hi back. It wasn't long until some of them began calling me by name, and by the end of the school year I knew almost everyone who went up and down the hall at the same time as I did.

The second helpful thing I learned was to focus on the person I was with and show a genuine interest in him or her. It is fun to get people talking about themselves; they love to do so.

The third helpful suggestion was to look for and put into words the positive qualities I saw in my friends. I learned never to put them down, even jokingly. People love to be around others who build them up. Learning to be a builder attracts people into your life.

I started following these suggestions, and the results were fantastic! I began making many friends. However, I still wasn't in a group I could call best friends. I didn't feel totally secure yet.

I turned sixteen during this time, and received my patriarchal blessing. I came to the patriarch's office in an attitude of fasting and prayer. As he laid his hands upon my head, he said many beautiful things. But one statement especially impressed me at this time. The patriarch didn't know me; he didn't know I was struggling with my friendships. However, he said, "Diane, choose friends who will bring spirituality to you, for some will become eternal friends. Hence their association will continue hereafter."

As he spoke these words, I had a peaceful feeling. In my mind I could see the face of a girl, and I immediately knew the group of people whose friendships I should cultivate at school. It was a large group of boys and girls who were involved in seminary, and some of them were in my classes.

But it is one thing to know what group you are to be a part of, and quite another to suddenly become a part of that group. What do you do—go to school on Monday and say, "Hey you guys, it was revealed to me this weekend I am supposed to be a part of your group, so let me in!"? It doesn't work that way. Of course, I needed to win their confidence and friendship over a period of time.

I determined that on Monday I would go to school and be extra friendly and nice to them so they would want me to be a part of their group. I did exactly that. I was friendly to them, and they were friendly back. However, they were nice to everyone, and that didn't make me a part of their group.

One Friday afternoon, some of girls in the group were standing outside the Junior Choir room, talking about a party they were going to have that night at Deb's cabin—an overnighter just for the girls. It was the kind of party that might even end up in a testimony meeting. I ached to be asked to go.

I stood there, hoping someone would notice me and invite me to the party. Everyone was excited about what they were going to bring and do, but no one said a word to me about going.

I went home that Friday afternoon and once again threw myself on my bed and cried. Then I got on my knees and began to pray. I cried out to Heavenly Father with all the energy of a broken heart. I told him I had done everything within my power—everything I knew how to do. I had sought out this group of friends, but now I needed his help. "Please, Heavenly Father, wilt Thou help me over the gap?"

Heavenly Father heard my prayer. The following week at school, some of the girls in the group invited me to have lunch with them. A few days later, they invited me to study with them after school. Within a very short period of time I was completely integrated into the group.

Some months later, one of the girls in the group came to me and said, "Diane, I have something really special I want to share with you. Do you remember the night of Deb's cabin party?"

I said, "Do I ever! I cried my eyes out that night. I was really hurt that I hadn't been invited. I even got on my knees and prayed that I could be a part of your group."

She said, "Well, Heavenly Father heard your prayer. That night while we were at the cabin, a few of us went into another room just to talk. While I was walking down the hall, your name kept going over and over in my mind. I turned to the others and said I had this feeling we should have invited Diane to the party tonight. In fact, I said I felt Diane should be a part of our group." I will be eternally grateful to this spiritually sensitive young lady who went on to become one of my dearest friends.

At another time in my life, I was unknowingly the answer to someone else's prayer. Through a series of miracles we had found a home in a certain area in Salt Lake, and shortly after moving there I met and became good friends with a lovely sister. She later told me that she had felt a great need to find a close friend. She had not been able to find someone in her area with the same interests, so she had begun to pray for someone to move into her ward whom she could have as a close friend.

In only a short period of time, miracles occurred, we moved into the ward, and she and I quickly became good friends. The move filled our needs for a home, but it also helped my friend know that God was aware of her. Whether we are a parent or a child who needs a friend, or a parent who is hoping for a child to find some new friends, we can go to God and ask for his help.

The Powers of Heaven Can Reveal Insights and Understanding

A mother confided in me that she was very concerned about

her teenage daughter, who was doing things that were inappropriate to her age and her beliefs. This mother had reason to be worried and concerned.

One day as she prayed about this problem, she received an impression that she should talk with her bishop. She called and made an appointment. During their interview, the bishop gave her insights and understanding that proved to be exactly what she needed to solve the problems with her daughter. This mother learned that without a doubt, God was aware of her and her daughter.

Whether insights come through the quiet whisperings of the Spirit to the mind, or through another person, our Father will give us answers that are appropriate for us if we call on him in faith.

Another example of this principle occurred when I was preparing a series of talks for Education Week a few years ago. I felt I had been prompted to give a class on parental discipline. I was a young parent at the time; my oldest child was only five years old. I was certainly not seasoned with experience. I felt inadequate and wasn't convinced that I was the person to be teaching parents how to discipline their children. I thought someone else, who had more depth of experience than I—perhaps a mother with several children ranging in age from teenager to infant—should teach it. However, I continued to pray about the matter, and continued to feel distinctly that I was to present that class.

I titled the series of classes "Joy in Being a Parent." I also came up with titles for the individual classes. One was called "Discipline Made Easy." The titles were cleared through the Church Correlation Committee, and I began the research for them. As I was doing the research, I became concerned again. I worried that discipline was a tough subject to try to teach to people who knew so much more than I did.

However, I decided I would be thorough in my studies to make sure I gave the best advice possible. I studied all the books I could find on different forms of discipline. The more I studied, the more confused I became. One psychologist said one thing;

another said just the opposite. There was one contradiction after another, with each "expert" giving his or her personal view. Looking back, I think how naive I was to give a lecture using such a title as "Discipline Made Easy." Is discipline *ever* easy?

After a fair amount of study, I had a sweet and significant experience. I knelt and said, "Dear Father, I have felt prompted to do this class on parental discipline. I feel inadequate and unskilled in this area. Wilt thou please help me? I have read many differing views, some contradicting the others. Wilt thou please let me know the best way for us to guide our children and to discipline when necessary?"

As I prayed, I felt a unique concept enlighten my mind. This concept covered parenting, discipline, and teaching and training children, as well as handling difficult situations with love, patience, and long-suffering.

While still on my knees, I felt overwhelmed with the insights that flooded into my mind. I felt deeply humbled. I knew I could never have come up with these ideas on my own, and I was certain that these insights were not found, as a whole, in any of the research I had done.

The concepts I taught in that Education Week series did not come from me. They were insights from the Spirit. After the class, many people said that as I shared the concepts with them, it was an "Aha" experience; the ideas fell into place with concepts they could see would work, and which made perfect sense.

The Powers of Heaven Can Protect Us or Warn Us of Danger

I was serving as a missionary in Arras, France in the winter of 1981—the coldest winter France had had in twenty years. We were riding our bikes from one area to another many miles every day. To help protect ourselves from the bitter cold, we put on layers of clothes, warm gloves, and sturdy boots.

One day it was especially cold. The humidity was high, the temperature was below freezing, the wind was strong, and there was a fair amount of snow on the ground. Our feet felt frozen, and we could hardly feel the fingers in our gloves.

I don't recall ever feeling as cold in my life as I did at that moment. Tears began to stream down my face. I didn't know if I could go any further, but we had an important appointment to meet.

In my moment of despair, I cried out to heaven for help. As I prayed, my body began to warm. The warm feeling started at my heart, like a burning that swelled within my abdomen and warmed my inner core. It extended to each of my limbs, to the tips of my fingers and the tips of my toes. It was as though there was a heater inside of me, heating my body as I rode along. Tears again filled my eyes; this time they were tears of gratitude and joy. At that moment, my testimony of God's tender care for us increased.

I remember another experience when a friend and I had traveled many hours to attend a wedding reception. In order to arrive before the reception was over, we had not stopped to eat on the way. We were famished and were counting on the refreshments to get us through the evening.

When we arrived, we went through the line and then hurried for the refreshment tables. When we sat down we saw that the caterers were putting everything away, and one of the servers told us the food was gone. We sat there hungry and disappointed, until we saw a big punchbowl across the room that was still full of punch. It appeared to have ice cream in it. We made a beeline for the table to get some before it disappeared, too.

My friend served up a cup of the slush for me, and then one for himself. As I lifted the glass to my mouth, something inside said, "Stop." I began to set the glass back down and was surprised to see my friend was doing the same thing. We were puzzled about the prompting until the father of the groom came across the room and said, "You probably don't want to drink that—it's loaded with alcohol!"

Neither of us had smelled the alcohol, and we were both extremely thirsty and hungry, so it was not logic that had caused us to obey when the Spirit had spoken to our minds.

The Powers of Heaven Can Lift a Heavy Heart

Years ago, I heard a woman relate the experience of having one of her teenage children go astray. This child had done something terribly wrong and shameful. The mother said she had fallen to her knees hurting, sorrowing, and weeping bitter tears as she cried out to the Lord. She testified, "I felt the arms of the Lord reach around me and embrace me."

When our hearts are heavy, our Father and his Son are deeply aware. In 3 Nephi, the Savior clearly expresses our Father's desire to help us:

> Ask, and it shall be given unto you; seek, and ye shall find; knock, and it shall be opened unto you.
>
> For every one that asketh, receiveth; and he that seeketh, findeth; and to him that knocketh, it shall be opened.
>
> Or what man is there of you, who, if his son ask bread, will give him a stone?
>
> Or if he ask a fish, will he give him a serpent?
>
> If ye then, being evil, know how to give good gifts unto your children, how much more shall your Father who is in heaven give good things to them that ask him? (3 Nephi 13:7-11)

Not long ago, I became acquainted with a wonderful single mother who has great faith. On several occasions she has shared some of her life's experiences with me. She has gone through many trials in her life, including losing a child in death.

She was now in the midst of another trial, this one more grievous and difficult than all the others. She related the following experience to me. She was lying on her bed, feeling so deeply burdened that she could hardly lift herself from her bed as she pleaded for help from Heavenly Father.

My friend said she had heard that one could pray for comfort from angels. She cried out for that kind of comfort. While praying, her spiritual eyes were opened. She saw her room fill with angels who surrounded her, and she sensed that the son she had lost was among them. She basked in the warmth and love that surrounded her, feeling comfort and peace beyond words.

After a time, the angelic visitors began to leave. She called out to them, "I know you have to go now, but could my son stay a little longer?" As she spoke those words, she felt her son put his hands on top of hers. He stayed with her and comforted her for a few minutes longer. This experience gave her the strength to go on and meet her challenges with faith and hope.

Sometimes our heavy hearts are caused by experiences that we are unable to change. Such was the case with another woman I met a number of years ago. After a women's conference where I had spoken, she shared with me the hope she had always had to have a large family. But she had many difficulties during pregnancies. She would become so ill that her body would become physically dehydrated, and she would end up in the hospital.

She bore two children, but both pregnancies were terribly difficult. The second took such a heavy physical toll on her that her husband told her he did not want them to have any more children. She struggled with this because of her longing for a large family. As time went on, her husband became even more adamant about this issue, and it caused marital discord between them.

One day, the pain of not having more children was so great that she went into a private room in their home, fell to her knees, and began to pray. An overwhelming sense of peace came over her, and she shared her experience of feeling the love of our heavenly parents. She could see them in her mind putting their arms around her. Then into her mind came the words: "We love you so much. It is enough that you desire to have children. You will be greatly blessed because of the desires of your heart."

Two thousand years ago, the Savior spoke of the peace he can give to us—a peace that is not of this world:

> Peace I leave with you, my peace I give unto you; not
> as the world giveth, give I unto you. Let not your heart
> be troubled, neither let it be afraid. (John 14:27)

The Powers of Heaven Can Help Us Find Things

A group of teenagers lost an expensive water ski. They had been searching the lake, but they were having no luck. One of the teens suggested that they pray about it.

"Heavenly Father doesn't have time to be bothered with helping us look for the ski," Dave said. "He has a lot more important things to do. We'll just have to find it on our own." Reluctantly they docked, loaded up their belongings, and left the lake to go home.

Should we ask for help to find things we have lost? Should such seemingly trivial, daily concerns be brought before our Father in prayer?

It is my experience that our Father wants to help us in *all* areas of our lives. As we turn our thoughts toward him, we make him a part of every aspect of our day. He will help us if we humbly ask him, including those frustrating moments when we may lose something.

It is perplexing to lose something, make a grand search, and still not find it. For example, one day Chris was looking for an important document he had misplaced. He needed it desperately. He had looked everywhere—in cupboards, filing cabinets, desk drawers, and on bookshelves. He had given it his best effort, but he knew that there was one source he had not used. He decided to call upon the powers of heaven. Humbly, he knelt and asked

Heavenly Father for help.

As he prayed his mind was opened, and he could see exactly where that paper was—in the third file drawer of a certain filing cabinet, under a stack of papers. He immediately went to the filing cabinet, opened the third drawer, and fingered through the stack of papers. Sure enough, there was the document, under the stack of papers. He gratefully fell to his knees in a prayer of thanks.

Small miracles can and will take place in our lives, and our faith will continually be strengthened if we make God a part of our lives and let him help us in our daily activities.

Over the years, Chris and I have made a diligent effort to teach our children to ask Heavenly Father for help. I am amazed at how many times they do petition him in prayer to help them find lost items. Doing so has strengthened their faith tremendously, because it seems that every time they pray about something they have misplaced, they find it.

I love to tell them the story of a young child whose father lost his wallet. He had torn his room apart looking in drawers, pant pockets, briefcases, and under beds. As the child listened to his frustration, she went into her bedroom and knelt in prayer. She asked Heavenly Father to help them find her dad's wallet because it was important to him.

When she got up from her knees, she joined the family's search to help find the wallet. She knew in her heart that Heavenly Father would help them. Shortly after that prayer, she opened a drawer and found it. Her father was surprised; he had looked in that drawer several times without seeing it. She knew, as a very young child, that God had helped her find that wallet.

Many years ago, I had a faith-building experience where drawing on the powers of heaven helped me to find something. I was washing the dishes one day when I happened to glance down and notice that the diamond in my solitaire engagement ring was gone. In horror, I informed Chris. He told me the diamond itself was worth thousands of dollars, and we wouldn't be able to replace it for a long time. He suggested that I search our home to see if I could find it.

In tears, I called my mother. She suggested I begin my search by putting a clean bag in the vacuum and vacuuming every inch of our home, then cutting the bag open and going through it with a razor blade.

I began my search, but periodically I went up to my bedroom to pray for help in finding the diamond. I told Heavenly Father that it was a very expensive diamond, and I asked him to *please* help me find it. I continued to search, but I did not find it. I wondered if Heavenly Father was hearing my prayer. I spent hours searching and praying, but with no success.

As the day wore on, I realized that in praying and trying to find the diamond, my whole emphasis had been focused on its material worth. My heart had been set on the things of the world. A gradual change began to take place inside my heart.

After vacuuming every square inch of our home, every article of clothing, and every bed, couch, and chair, I fell to my knees and asked for forgiveness. "Father, my heart has been wrong today," I said. "I have had it set upon worldly things. Please forgive me. I can understand why I have not found the diamond. Through the course of this day my heart has been humbled, and I feel I can live without the diamond. I can accept that it is gone. The ring does have sentimental value to me because it was my engagement ring. If in thine infinite wisdom, thou dost feel that my heart is right and it is right for me to have the diamond back, wilt thou help me find it? If not, then I will understand." My heart had truly changed.

Within just a few moments after offering that prayer of humility, I spotted the diamond. I found it behind the door in the laundry room, where it had probably flown from my ring as I was shaking out clothes before dropping them into the washing machine. I felt humbled and grateful to know that my Heavenly Father had heard my prayers, and even more humbled to know that the intent of our hearts makes a difference when we call upon the powers of heaven.

On November 16, 1986, the story of a four-year-old Arizona girl named Sarah Skidmore, who had been kidnapped, appeared in the *Church News*. On October 7, Sarah was pulled from a car parked in front of an elementary school in East Mesa. Police were contacted immediately, and search efforts began. Church members organized fasts, and people of many faiths in the area prayed for help. Youth passed out flyers to notify others of the kidnapping. Sarah's family held a press conference asking for the safe return of their daughter.

The night Sarah was kidnapped, her father gave his wife a priesthood blessing. "I was somewhat frightened to give the blessing," he remembered, "because I was really sad and didn't know if my emotional state would interfere with my feeling the Spirit." However, he added, "We said a prayer that I would know the words to say and that the Spirit of the Lord would guide me."

As he placed his hands on Rhonda's head and began to give the blessing, he told her that she was not to feel guilty about anything. He also told his wife to be patient and faithful. "Finally," he added, "I had a very firm confirmation that Sarah would be okay. I blessed Rhonda with the knowledge that Sarah had many more important things to do in this life and there was no power that would be able to harm her. I told Rhonda that angels were attending Sarah and supporting her."

After the blessing, Sarah's father felt overwhelmed by emotion. "I knew she would be protected from the elements and would not suffer for food or water," he recalled. "I knew she would come back to us and grow up in our home."

On October 10, hunters found Sarah wandering in a desert wash near Saguaro Lake, about ten miles outside of Mesa. She was taken to a hospital emergency room, where she was examined by doctors. She showed no signs of recognizing her parents and appeared to be in a daze.

Eventually, Sarah began talking about the experience. She said she had seen her two-year-old sister Heather (who was safe at home) playing in the desert, building a rock pile. "When the rocks fell down," Sarah told her parents, "I laughed and laughed and laughed. And whenever I got scared, I could see Heather playing with the rocks and I wasn't afraid anymore." Later Sarah told her parents the girl she had seen playing in the desert was not Heather, but a small, blonde girl who looked like her sister.

For two days and two nights, Sarah stayed near some trees, which gave her shelter from the rain. At home, her parents were praying she would stay dry and find shelter.

Eventually, Sarah left the shelter of the trees. She told her parents she knew where to walk because she followed a sidewalk that led her out of the desert to where the hunters found her.

"Are there sidewalks in the desert?" Sarah's father asked his daughter.

"Not *in* the desert, going *out* of the desert," Sarah replied. (Article written by Sarah Heims for the *Church News,* Nov. 16, 1986, p. 12. Expanded version appears in *Coming From the Light* [New York: Pocket Books, Division of Simon and Schuster], to be released January 1997. Used by permission.)

The powers of Heaven *can* and *do* help us find things—and people—that are lost.

On the subject of prayer, Elder Bruce R. McConkie said, "Let us learn how to do so [pray] boldly and efficaciously, not in word only but in spirit and in power, so that we may pull down upon ourselves, even as he did upon himself, the very powers of heaven" (*Ensign,* Jan. 1976, p. 9. Used by permission.)

Each of us can receive great blessings in our daily lives if we live as righteously as we can and pull down the powers of heaven in our behalf by praying with great faith. Heavenly Father will guide us and assist us to receive the righteous desires of our hearts.

In a conference address in 1976, Elder Bruce R. McConkie stated that "When needs vary, so does the intensity of prayers." Then, referring to the Savior in the Garden of Gethsemane, he quoted Luke 22:44: "And being in an agony he prayed more earnestly: and his sweat was as it were great drops of blood falling down to the ground."

"Now here is a marvelous thing," Elder McConkie continued. "Note it well."

> The Son of God "prayed more earnestly"! He who did all things well . . . teaching us, his brethren, that all prayers, his included, are not alike, and that a greater need calls forth more earnest and faithful pleadings before the throne of him to whom the prayers of the Saints are a sweet savor. (*Ensign*, Jan. 1976, p. 8. Used by permission.)

The scriptures teach us that we should "counsel with the Lord" in all things. In speaking to his son, the prophet Alma gave this advice:

> Oh remember, my son, and learn wisdom in thy youth; yea, learn in thy youth to keep the commandments of God.
>
> Yea, and cry unto God for all thy support; yea let all thy doings be unto the Lord, and whithersoever thou goest let it be in the Lord; yea, let thy thoughts be directed unto the Lord; yea, let the affections of thy heart be placed upon the Lord forever.
>
> Counsel with the Lord in all thy doings, and he will direct thee for good; yea, when thou liest down at night lie down unto the Lord, that he may watch over you in your sleep; and when thou risest in the morning let thy heart be full of thanks unto God; and if ye do these things, ye shall be lifted up at the last day. (Alma 37:35-37)

Chapter Five

REPLACING FEAR WITH FAITH

During the mid-1970s, my mother's uncle passed away. She traveled to Idaho to attend the funeral, accompanied by my brother, Richard. They spent all day Saturday in Idaho visiting with family members and close friends. By the time they left it was late at night, and they had a four-hour drive ahead.

After driving for about three hours, Mom happened to glance down at the gas gauge. To her horror, the gauge registered empty. She had been so caught up in the events of the day that she had failed to check her gas supply. When she happened to look at the gauge, she was at Farmington, Utah—still a forty-five minute drive to her home in southeast Salt Lake. She knew from experience that the car she was driving had no leeway on the gas register. When it registered empty, it meant *empty!*

In the 1970s, during the gasoline crunch, gas stations closed early in the evening. Mom frantically scanned each freeway exit she passed, but there was not an all-night gas station to be seen.

Mom startled my brother by saying, "Richard, wake up. We have an emergency! We've got to do something fast, or we'll be stranded."

They decided to pray. Richard said the prayer as they drove along. He sincerely petitioned for help from above. As soon as he concluded the prayer, an overwhelming impression came to Mom: "Drive on. Do not look at the gas gauge." So she did.

She drove on, looking straight ahead, from Farmington to Bountiful, from Bountiful to North Salt Lake, from North Salt Lake to Salt Lake, and from Salt Lake to South Salt Lake, where she got off at the Interstate exchange and headed east toward

Holladay. She had now traveled for nearly forty minutes since their prayer had been offered.

Tears streamed down her cheeks. Her heart was full of joy. Mom knew that her car had been running on faith. "I was almost overcome with gratitude," she told me later. "At that instant, I don't know why, but as I neared home, I looked down at the gas gauge." The moment her mind registered that the gauge was still on empty, the car choked and then stopped completely dead.

Mother knew that her car had run out of gas forty minutes earlier, but because she had trusted the words spoken to her mind, the car had carried them to a safe distance from home.

The powers of heaven are governed by faith. Joseph Smith teaches us three things concerning the nature of faith:

> (1) . . . as faith is the moving cause of all action in temporal concerns, so it is in spiritual;
> (2) Faith is not only the principle of action, but of power also,
> (3) Faith, then, is the first great governing principle which has power, dominion, and authority over all things. (*Lectures on Faith*. Salt Lake City: Deseret Book Company, 1985, pp. 8-9.)

On March 4, 1990, in a fireside address given at Brigham Young University, Elder Boyd K. Packer recalled going to Elder Harold B. Lee for counsel shortly after being called as a General Authority. He listened carefully to Elder Packer's problem and suggested that he see President David O. McKay. President McKay counseled Elder Packer, and, Elder Packer recalled, he was willing to obey but saw no possible way to do as President McKay had counseled him:

> I returned to Elder Lee and told him that I saw no way to move in the direction I was counseled to go. He said, "The trouble with you is you want to see the end

from the beginning." I replied that I would like to see at least a step or two ahead. Then came the lesson of a lifetime: "You must learn to walk to the edge of the light, and then a few steps into the darkness; then the light will appear and show the way before you." Then he quoted these words from the Book of Mormon: "Dispute not because ye see not, for ye receive no witness until after the trial of your faith" (Ether 12:6) Those eighteen words from Moroni have been like a beacon light to me. (*BYU Today*, vol. 45, no. 2, March 1991, pp. 22-23.)

Another powerful message about faith is found in Doctrine and Covenants 67:3:

Ye endeavored to believe that ye should receive the blessing which was offered unto you; but behold, verily I say unto you there were fears in your hearts, and verily this is the reason that ye did not receive.

When we have fears in our hearts, we deny ourselves the blessings of heaven. But when we replace our fears with faith, the powers of heaven can be brought down in our behalf.

I had a personal experience with this principle. After I had spent a number of years at home as a full-time mom, some unusual circumstances occurred in the seminar industry (which provided our income) that caused severe strain on our finances. Postal rates jumped, causing us to pay tens of thousands of dollars more in postal costs with each advertising campaign. Little by little our profits were being skimmed off, leaving little for us to live on.

Chris came home one night very discouraged. He said, "Diane, I hate to tell you this, but you're going to have to go back to work."

After dropping that bombshell, Chris had to leave for a meeting. I was left alone with my little children to think about what he had just said.

I put the children to bed. In my heart I agonized over having to go back to work, even though I understood the dire financial circumstances we were in. I wasn't upset about having to find a job; I had taught school, spoken professionally, and done secretarial work and career counseling, so getting a job would be easy enough. I was agonizing because of my children. I couldn't bear the thought of taking them to a day-care center and leaving them each day, but it seemed there was no other solution to our dilemma.

I went into my living room to pray. I desperately wanted guidance, and I poured out my heart with every fiber of my being. I pleaded with Heavenly Father to know his will concerning my life, and I told him I would do whatever it was. I had decided if the answer was that I should go back to work, I would do that; but if Heavenly Father wanted me to stay home, I would do that, no matter what financial sacrifices we had to make. As I poured out my heart in prayer that night, an answer finally came.

When Chris arrived home later that evening, I was in a very tender mood. I went to him and said gently, "I have something important to tell you. I've been on my knees tonight praying. I asked Heavenly Father to let me know his will concerning our lives right now. He knows our circumstances. He knows the heavy burdens we carry. I asked him what he would have me do. The answer he gave me is to stay home. He wants me to be with the children and *not* go back to work. He also let me know that everything will be all right financially. I don't know how, but he gave me the comfort and the peace to know that all will be well with us, and that miracles will take place financially."

I looked at Chris and, with a twinkle in my eye, I said, "But don't take my word for it. Why don't you get on your knees and do whatever it takes for you to find out his will as well?"

Chris said, "Oh, Diane, I believe you."

Chris and I took a few steps into the darkness, and then the light began to show the way before us. In a period of a few weeks, miracles did begin to take place in our lives. Doors opened, opportunities came, and the financial wherewithal became available to make it possible for me to stay at home and continue to be a full-time mother.

When we face trials or challenges, getting on our knees and *staying there* until we feel the Spirit can be the key to having our fears replaced with faith. As we pray humbly, the fear will dissipate and our faith will grow.

Elder Bruce R. McConkie stated that "Faith is a gift of God bestowed as a reward for personal righteousness. It is always given when righteousness is present and the greater the measure of obedience to God's laws the greater will be the endowment of faith" (*Mormon Doctrine.* Salt Lake City: Deseret Book Company, 1966, p. 264).

I would like to share some experiences in which fear was replaced by faith. In each case, the people involved turned to the true source of strength. In doing so, they were able to face their challenges and carry their burdens, with God's help.

Before I had children, I was a speaker on the professional lecture circuit. I traveled from city to city, giving six-hour seminars. One week my mother came with me to see if she, too, would like to become a professional speaker.

We flew to Michigan, picked up a rental car, and continued to travel and speak for five consecutive days in Michigan and Indiana. On Thursday we arrived at our hotel in Grand Rapids, Michigan, unpacked, and began preparations for the morning.

Quite suddenly, I felt a fever coming on. I soon felt so sick that I didn't want to have dinner; I just wanted to go to bed. I got sicker and sicker, and before long I could hardly move.

I was deeply concerned about the next day's seminar. I was to speak to a capacity crowd of business professionals in a large hotel ballroom for six hours. It was a seminar I had given many times before, but at this point I was so sick I could hardly lift my head. I looked at my mother and said, "Mom, you may have to give the seminar for me tomorrow."

Fear struck her heart! She was only slightly acquainted with
the seminar. She hadn't studied it, and had only heard it a few
times. She had very little speaking experience—mostly giving
talks in church or conducting church meetings. She looked at me
and said, "Diane, I *can't!*"

I said, "Mom, I can't make it out on the stage tomorrow, and
all those people have paid good money to come. You can do it.
Look over the outline in my briefcase." Then I drifted off to sleep.

That night my mother, whose heart was full of fear, knelt by
my bed and began to pray. She poured out her heart, pleaded for
forgiveness for anything she had ever done wrong in her life, and
literally turned her life over to God. She recommitted her life to
him, and then humbly asked him to make me well.

Mom prayed for many hours as I slept. Then, spiritually,
physically, and emotionally drained, she climbed into the other
bed and fell asleep.

The next thing I remember was seeing the beautiful rays of
sunlight shining through the window. I sat up in my bed and
exclaimed, "Mom, Mom—wake up, wake up! You won't believe
this, but I feel good. I never get well this fast, but I honestly feel
good."

Tears welled in her eyes. I did not know then that she had
stayed up most of the night pleading with God to heal me.

In Doctrine and Covenants 8:10 we read, "Remember that
without faith you can do nothing; therefore ask in faith."

A friend shared with me a faith-building experience she had.
Her husband had been a successful business owner, and they had
lived comfortably for many years. However, through a series of
unfortunate circumstances, he lost the prosperous business he had
created.

They went through a very difficult period when they were on
the verge of bankruptcy and were about to lose everything they
had spent their lives to build. The experience caused my friend's
husband to sink into a deep depression.

One night during this time of trauma, my friend fell by the

side of her bed and pleaded with the Lord with all her heart for some relief from the terrible fear of the future she felt. She was overwhelmed with their financial situation, and did not know where they would get the money they needed even for the basic necessities of life. As she prayed, she felt the tender promptings of the Spirit. These sweet words were spoken to her mind:

> And why take ye thought for raiment? Consider the lilies of the field, how they grow; they toil not, neither do they spin; . . .
> Therefore take no thought, saying, What shall we eat? or, What shall we drink? or, Wherewithal shall we be clothed? . . .
> For your heavenly Father knoweth that ye have need of all these things.
> But seek ye first the kingdom of God, and his right-eousness, and all these things shall be added unto you.
> Take therefore no thought for the morrow, for the morrow shall take thought for the things of itself. . . .
> (3 Nephi 13:28, 31-34)

As these words filled her mind, she realized that God was mindful of her and her family's needs at that time. Her fear was replaced by faith.

Faith can replace fear and peace can come even as we are experiencing our trials. Peace comes from aligning our lives with what God desires us to do. We must find out God's will for us, then let go of the things that are not important and focus on the things he would have us do.

As we put our lives in alignment with the Lord's will and spend our time doing what he wants us to do, we will experience increasingly greater amounts of peace. As we raise our voices, our thoughts, and our hearts to heaven, the powers therein will comfort us and calm our fears.

A woman in Arizona shared with me how she was led to meet

her husband. She was in her late twenties, concerned, worried, and fearful as to whether she would marry. She had decided she wanted to go to graduate school. As she prayed about it, she felt impressed to apply to a school in a city in a completely different state than she had considered. She was not even aware of a school in that state, and she had to do some research to find the name of the university. After she learned the name of the school, whenever she thought about it she had a sweet, peaceful feeling. She applied to the graduate program and was accepted.

She had not been at the school very long when she met the young man who was to become her eternal companion. She often expresses gratitude for the promptings she received that led her to him.

In Mosiah 7:19-20, King Limhi counsels his people to

> Lift up your heads, and rejoice, and put your trust in God, in that God who was the God of Abraham, and Isaac, and Jacob; and also, that God who brought the children of Israel out of the land of Egypt, and caused that they should walk through the Red Sea on dry ground, and fed them with manna that they might not perish in the wilderness; and many more things did he do for them.
>
> And again, that same God has brought our fathers out of the land of Jerusalem, and has kept and preserved his people even until now.

The scriptures are replete with examples of how God has helped people overcome their fear and grow in faith. Just as he did for those in Biblical and Book of Mormon times, he will help us now.

Della Barnes, a lovely ninety-two-year-old woman, bore testimony of this principle. She was recovering from a stroke, and one night she lay on her bed feeling deep concern. She wondered whether her first husband, to whom she had been sealed in the temple but who had been dead for almost forty-five years, would still want her to be his companion after all the years they had been apart.

With fear in her heart, she raised her voice in prayer. She shared with me how her beloved companion came to her in the stillness of the night and embraced her. He told her to be comforted—that it wouldn't be long until they would be together again. Della's heart rejoiced; her fear was replaced with faith. A few months later, she passed from this life to the other side to join her companion.

God cares about our daily concerns. He wants to help us—but he has given us our agency. He wants us to humbly petition him, and to always express gratitude for the blessings he sends.

There is one important question we should ask ourselves when we are not experiencing the peace we desire: "Am I holding back anything from the Lord? Is there something he has guided me to do that I am not doing?" We are all at different stages in our spiritual development, and our circumstances are different. These are questions that only each individual and the Lord can answer.

I recall vividly a time in my life when I was holding back. I hardly realized that I was resisting the direction I was receiving from the Lord. Through the experience, I was humbled and learned several important lessons.

Shortly after Chris and I got married, we moved to Denver, Colorado, to set up our first home. Since I was in my late twenties, we wanted to start our family within a short time. I had taught school for several years before we were married, so we decided that I should teach until our first baby came.

To my disappointment, I found out that in order to be licensed to teach in Colorado, I would have to attend college for a year. Therefore, we decided that I should use my secretarial skills in a business career until we could have a baby. However, although we very much wanted a child, I was not able to conceive.

While we waited, I kept busy and gained a fair amount of experience in business. I also attended many business seminars.

Every time I went to a seminar, I came away positively motivated—not so much by the information being presented, as by what the seminar lecturer was doing. I wanted to lecture! It wasn't a spur-of-the-moment thought; it was a secret desire I had entertained for years.

After discussing the matter with Chris at length, I decided to take the big plunge. I contacted a national seminar company and enthusiastically pursued a speaking career. After numerous interviews, I was finally hired. Within a year I was on the national seminar circuit, traveling from city to city, speaking to hundreds of people a week and thoroughly loving it. I had found my niche. It was a lifelong dream coming true.

Chris and I had been married now for several years, and I received tremendous support from him. He was one of my greatest fans. Not only that, but he became interested in the seminar business himself and decided that he, too, wanted to become involved in this type of work.

His expertise was in management, operations, sales, and financial work. Mine was in writing and speaking. We combined our talents and started our own professional seminar training business. I would write the seminars and present them. He would do all the behind-the-scenes work of management, advertising, computerization, and operations.

We took all the money we had saved, borrowed more, and had the start-up capital necessary to begin our national seminar training company.

After all the investments were made and everything was in full swing, I found out I was pregnant with our first child! I was absolutely thrilled. I was in my thirties and having my first baby. In 1986 I gave birth to our first child, a beautiful baby girl, whom we named Whitney Anne. We were joyously happy to have a new baby in our home after waiting and hoping and praying for so long. I experienced a depth of fulfillment I had not yet known.

However, it seemed like everything was happening at once—a new baby *and* a new company. Years earlier, we had planned that as soon as we started our family, I would be able to stay at home. But since Whitney had been born so soon after we had started the company, it wasn't possible for me to quit working immediately. I still needed to write seminars and test them around the country to determine the best seminars to market. We couldn't afford to hire another writer or speaker to take my place.

While my baby slept during the day and at night, I wrote seminars. When Whitney was awake, Chris and I both spent time caring for the needs of our little one. We even arranged to have the office close to our home, complete with a cradle, so I could spend her nap time there.

When Chris and I traveled, we took Whitney with us. Chris's mother cared for Whitney while we were involved with the seminars, and we were with her in the evenings.

At first it worked out fine. Then we began traveling more, Whitney grew, and Chris's parents were called on a mission. I felt torn. I was the only person who knew the material in the seminars I had written, and yet I was the one who needed and wanted to be home full-time with my precious child. Financially it didn't seem possible yet.

That year, President Ezra Taft Benson spoke to the mothers of Zion saying,

> Now my dear mothers, knowing of your divine role to bear and rear children and bring them back to Him, how will you accomplish this in the Lord's way? I say the "Lord's way," because it is different from the world's way.
>
> The Lord clearly defined the roles of mothers and fathers in providing for the rearing of a righteous posterity. In the beginning, Adam—not Eve—was instructed to earn the bread by the sweat of his brow. Contrary to conventional wisdom, a mother's calling is in the home, not in the marketplace.
>
> . . . the counsel of the Church has always been for

mothers to spend their full time in the home in rearing and caring for their children. ("To the Mothers in Zion," pamphlet, Salt Lake City: Corporation of the President, 1987, p. 5. Used by permission.)

I knew in my heart as President Benson spoke that he was inspired of God. He continued:

We realize also that some of our choice sisters are widowed and divorced and that others find themselves in unusual circumstances where, out of necessity, they are required to work for a period of time. But these instances are the exception, not the rule." ("To the Mothers in Zion," p. 6. Used by permission.)

"He said 'unusual circumstances.' Yes, mine is an unusual circumstance," I thought. "Surely I am one of those exceptions he spoke of. After all, the Lord knows we've invested large sums of money into this company, and he knows how expensive it would be to hire a speaker in my place." I felt consoled for a time.

Meanwhile, the prophet's words had impressed me with such force that I began writing a seminar for professional working women on the importance of family relationships. I decided I would teach professional businesswomen around the country (mostly non-LDS) to put their first priorities back on their families rather than on their careers. It took some prayerful preparation and careful wording to present such a seminar. I prayed fervently and felt the Spirit of the Lord guiding me as I put together the materials.

I was pleased with the final results, and soon began testing the program around the country. I received an overwhelmingly positive response. Many women came to me in tears at the end of the sessions. Others gave me hugs and whispered, "Thank you." I became aware that *all* working mothers had frustrations. Many women asked for advice and direction.

I, however, found myself in a hypocritical situation. I, too, felt all the frustrations, guilt, and uneasiness other working mothers faced each day. Yet here I was, teaching women to spend more time with their families, and yet I was spending time away from my family to do so!

Even though I had originally thought I was the exception to the prophet's counsel because of our unusual circumstances, I knew deep down in my heart that I wasn't. In some ways I felt that perhaps I had been holding back from the Lord—not because I wanted to, but because I had let circumstances dictate the outcome rather than exercising more faith. I knew I needed to be at home full-time, even though I had found the perfect outside career.

A good friend told me that at the time the prophet gave his talk "To the Mothers of Zion," her husband was out of work. She got on her knees that night, expressed her love and faith, and then humbly asked Heavenly Father for help.

The next day, she demonstrated her faith by putting in her two-weeks' notice at work. I remember thinking, "She, of all people, surely had the 'unusual circumstances' the prophet spoke of to justify working. But she chose instead to follow the prophet. What faith! Now they will have no income."

God rewarded her faithfulness. Within a short time, her husband was offered an excellent job—one of the best he had had. I deeply appreciated this dear friend's example of faith.

The words of Nephi flooded my mind. Each time he was given something difficult to do, he put his trust in the Lord:

> And it came to pass that I, Nephi, said unto my father: I will go and do the things which the Lord hath commanded, for I know that the Lord giveth no commandments unto the children of men, save he shall prepare a way for them that they may accomplish the thing which he commandeth them. (1 Ne. 3:7)

Later, Nephi told his brothers,

> If God had commanded me to do all things I could
> do them. If he should command me that I should say
> unto this water, be thou earth, it should be earth; and
> if I should say it, it would be done.
> And now, if the Lord has such great power, and has
> wrought so many miracles among the children of men,
> how is it that he cannot instruct me, that I should
> build a ship? (1 Ne. 17:50-51)

I thought, "Diane, where is your faith? If the Lord commands
you to be at home with your family, why are you not doing it?"

I prayed humbly, "Heavenly Father, I do not know how it is
possible for me to quit working, but I am going to put my faith
in thee. Please, wilt thou help me?"

I knew if I had enough faith, God could provide the way for
me to be at home with my daughter to fulfill the commandment
he had given.

There was no more questioning in my heart. I had two more
tours of seminars to give, and I decided that after that, I would
quit for good. I would continue to pray humbly for help from
above—first, to find a really good seminar lecturer and second, to
open a way for Chris and me to be able to pay this person.

I wanted to hire a woman, since my seminar was for mothers.
I wanted her to be professional in dress and manner, since she
would be speaking to professional women. I also wanted someone
who was dynamic, energetic, and natural on stage—someone with
a good amount of speaking experience. I wanted to hire a woman
whose family was raised so she wouldn't have the same dilemma I
faced in being away from home. Finally, she needed to be religious, since I was teaching a seminar that promoted traditional
Christian values.

On the next seminar tour, I was speaking at the Hilton in
Pasadena, California. Some of the women in the audience invited

me to have lunch with them. I usually go to my hotel room to rest during my lunch hour, but this time I thought, "Why not?"

One of the women at the table said, "It must be hard to leave your little daughter." I choked up; she had zeroed in on my tender spot. "That is my biggest dilemma," I said. "I am looking for someone to take my place so I can be at home with her."

Another woman at the table, Val, turned to me and said, "You know, I've got the perfect woman to teach your seminar. Her speaking experience is in this very area of family relations."

My ears perked up. Numerous people had expressed an interest in working for us, but few of them had any speaking experience. Val told me more about her friend, and I knew I wanted to meet her. "The only problem is that she lives in Phoenix," Val said.

"You're not going to believe this," I said enthusiastically, "but tomorrow I'm doing a seminar in Phoenix. Call your friend, and have her come to the hotel to meet me."

When I arrived in Phoenix, I received a call from Val's friend. She was the president of a business and had too many pressures to get away that day. She told me she would send me a copy of her resume. "Oh, well," I thought, "it was a good idea, anyway."

Toward the end of the day, I received a message asking me to contact this woman immediately. When I called she said, "Don't leave. I'm on my way over to meet you."

I was waiting in the hotel lobby when Euna came through the doors. Even before she spoke, the Spirit whispered to my heart. I knew she was our new speaker.

Right away I could see she was professional and energetic. She exuded confidence and was poised and polished in her manner. She had had twelve years of professional speaking experience, *and* her family was raised. Not only that, she was religious.

As we conversed, she explained to me how pressed for time she had been that day, and yet she had a persistent feeling that she should come and meet me. Then Euna said softly, "I feel like God sent me today."

"I know," I whispered.

We hired Euna shortly after that first meeting. She was an outstanding seminar lecturer for us. During those early months, we found out that she was one of the top female speakers in America. She has shared the stage with Zig Ziglar, Dr. Joyce Brothers, and other well-known speakers. She had been sought after by the top seminar companies, yet she decided to work for us.

I felt as if Heavenly Father had said, "Diane, because you have exercised faith in me, I will help you and bless you." And he has. Heavenly Father hand-picked one of the top speakers in America for our little company because of a mother's desire to be at home with her child!

After Euna started speaking for us, we began selling products at the seminars, and the profits from these sales more than paid for her salary as a speaker. The words of Nephi rang again in my ears: "For I know that the Lord giveth no commandments unto the children of men, save he shall prepare a way for them . . ." (1 Ne. 3:7).

Exercising faith in the Lord is a powerful principle. With Heavenly Father's help, I was able to be a greater part of my children's lives. I felt as though my life was in alignment with his will in this area. That assurance alone brought a great deal of peace, contentment, and joy into my life.

God cares about each of us. He understands our circumstances. Some women do have to work. If that is your circumstance, he will lighten your burden or help you find ways to be away from home for fewer hours.

If we have a desire to obey the Lord's commandments in any area, he will prepare a way for us to do so. As we learn to hold back nothing from him, he will hold back nothing from us. When we put our lives in alignment with his will, he will fill our lives with peace. As the scriptures say, "I, the Lord, am bound when ye do what I say; but when ye do not what I say, ye have no promise" (D&C 82:10).

Chapter Six

TOUCHING LIVES

One day as a man was walking along the seashore, be observed noticed that during the night many seashells and starfish had washed up on the shore. He was thoroughly enjoying the morning sun and the cool sea air, as he strolled for miles along the sand. Far off in the distance, the man noticed a figure joyfully celebrating life in a grand and uninhibited fashion.

He was curious as he watched, because it looked as if this person was dancing. As the man came closer, he could see it was a little girl picking up starfish that had washed upon the shore and throwing them, one by one, back into the surf.

He walked up to her and asked, "Why are you throwing those starfishback in the water?" The little child answered, "If I leave them on the beach, they'll die. I am throwing them back into the water so they can live."

The man was silent for a moment. He was impressed with the child's thoughtfulness, but was also aware of how futile her attempts to save the starfish were. He motioned up and down the miles and miles of beach and said to her, "There must be hundreds, even thousands of starfish along the beach. How can you possibly expect to make much of a difference?"

The young girl thought about the man's words for a moment, then reached down, picked up another starfish, and threw it into the water. She glanced back at the man and said, "You're probably right, but I just made a difference with *that* one." (Paraphrased from the original source, which is unknown.)

There are many needs around each of us. We cannot possibly "save all the starfish," but each of us can make a difference with one person at a time. We should begin with those in our immediate homes—those we spend every day with. We can make a significant difference in the lives of our spouses, our children, our parents, siblings and our extended families if we have a desire to do so.

Relationships can be fragile, but they are important. We have been told that the Holy Ghost will let us know all things that we should do. (See 2 Ne. 32:3.) Therefore, why not let the Spirit guide us in making a difference in our relationships with one another?

The Spirit can bless us when we are having disagreements or troubles in any of our relationships. One day several years ago, I was upset with my husband. I don't remember what we disagreed about, but I knew I was right and he was wrong. He knew *he* was right and *I* was wrong.

I had read somewhere that a person could ask Heavenly Father to change another person's heart. I went into the other room, in a disgusted frame of mind. I planned to get on my knees and ask Heavenly Father to change my husband's heart so he would see this issue the "right" way—*my* way.

As I got on my knees, I began to weep. "Oh, Father, forgive me," I said. "Wilt thou change my heart so I will understand my husband?" As I said those words, the Spirit filled my whole being. Heavenly Father softened my heart, and I was able to go back to my husband and discuss the issue with tenderness and kindness.

When we are struggling in any relationship, we can turn our hearts heavenward. We can go to a quiet spot and say, "Heavenly Father, help me with this child right now. Please give me the insights and inspiration to deal with this problem." We may ask for help in loving a child who gets on our nerves or a partner who is doing something we disagree with. We may pray, "Please help me to understand my parents," or "Please help me feel closer to my brothers and sisters."

If our hearts are filled with the Spirit, we can build and strengthen our relationships. When we are struggling or hurting, Nephi's words can remind us where to turn:

Yea, I know that God will give liberally to him that
asketh. Yea, my God will give me, if I ask not amiss;
therefore I will lift up my voice unto thee; yea, I will
cry unto thee, my God, the rock of my righteousness.
Behold, my voice shall forever ascend up unto thee, my
rock and mine everlasting God. Amen. (2 Ne. 4:35)

Our lives are made up of relationships. In addition to those
with our families and extended families, we also have relationships
with neighbors, friends, ward members, co-workers, and acquain-
tances.

As we build a close relationship with our Father in Heaven,
our love for ourselves grows, and our feelings of worth increase. As
we learn to feel good about who we are, our love for others grows
and our desires become more focused on being kind and loving to
others.

When Jesus was asked, "Master, which is the great commandment in the law?" he replied:

Thou shalt love the Lord thy God with all thy heart,
and with all thy soul, and with all thy mind.
This is the first and great commandment.
The second is like unto it, Thou shalt love thy neighbor as thyself.
On these two commandments hang all the law and
the prophets. (Matt. 22:35-40)

The way to true happiness in our lives is to build a close relationship with God, put him first in our lives, and then turn our
lives outward toward others. As the hymn puts it,

I would be my brother's keeper; I would learn the
healer's art.
To the wounded and the weary I would show a gentle heart.

I would be my brothers keeper—Lord, I would follow
Thee. (Hymns, no. 220)

Several years ago, I was in the fifth month of a pregnancy. I
was not feeling well one day and came home early from running
some errands. Things didn't feel quite right. Two years earlier I
had lost a baby in the fifth month of pregnancy, so I was worried.

As I checked myself, I discovered that my baby was coming! I
called to my husband, who had an office in our home. We called
the doctor, who told us to drive to the hospital as fast as we could.

Before we left for the hospital, I asked Chris to give me a
blessing. He did. As he prayed, an impression came to me that we
should call an ambulance rather than driving to the hospital ourselves.

We did not have insurance, and our finances were tight. For a
brief moment the costs passed through my mind, and then I said,
"Chris, we have to call an ambulance. As you gave me the blessing, it came to me that we must call an ambulance. If I go in the
car, the water sac will break, and the baby's chances of survival will
be gone."

He said, "Whatever we have to do, let's do it."

As they rolled me into emergency labor and delivery, a nurse
came in. She took one look at the situation and said, "This is serious. It's a good thing you called the ambulance. If you had driven
to the hospital, the water sac would have broken."

I offered a silent prayer of thanks. Heavenly Father had
known the precariousness of my situation, and the Spirit had
warned us. My doctor, who is a specialist in high-risk pregnancies,
took my husband aside and said, "Chris, this is very serious. It
looks like the baby is going to come tonight. If it does, the baby's
chances of surviving are about four percent."

I was rushed by ambulance to another hospital with a peri-
natal department. I spent many hours lying in an emergency
room with my head slanted down, in an attempt to get the sac to
go back in place. During that time I offered many prayers. In the

following days, weeks, and months, we were part of a miracle. Our baby's life was saved.

The doctor wanted me to stay in the hospital for four months, but we had no insurance and I had run up a good-sized bill in the week I had already been there. I negotiated with the doctor to let me go home so my family could take care of me. The doctor consented, on condition that I have someone there to take care of me at all times.

We were able to arrange for our family members and close friends to take turns caring for me. I stayed with one family and then another, going back and forth to different homes. I felt such deep gratitude for the tireless help and kindness expended in my behalf.

One week I was scheduled to stay at a particular home, but we found out that we had mis-communicated and the family was going to be out of town. I had no place to go with my children. I could only lie on the couch at my parents' home, feeling helpless and alone. I thought of calling my mother at work. She would have quit her job to come home and take care of me, but I couldn't ask that of her. I had already imposed on everyone so much that I just couldn't make myself call anyone to ask if I could come to stay again. I didn't know what to do, so I prayed. A short time later, the telephone rang. When I answered it, Marie James, my visiting teacher, said, "Diane, I have been trying all morning to find out where you are. Are you okay?"

I couldn't hold back the tears as I explained my awkward situation. "Oh, my Diane," she said, "don't you worry. Have Chris take you to your home; I will come over and take care of you today, and we'll get others to help for the coming days and weeks."

Marie came over and cared for me that day. She also made numerous phone calls, and within twenty-four hours my entire ward was mobilized to help me for the rest of my confinement. Women came and went, helping to take care of me every day for months. I experienced the most beautiful acts of charity I had seen in my life, and my life was greatly blessed.

We can all do as the hymn states in learning to follow the Savior:

> Savior, may I learn to love thee,
> Walk the path that Thou hast shown,
> Pause to help and lift another,
> Finding strength beyond my own.
> Savior, may I learn to love Thee—Lord, I would follow
> Thee. (Hymns, no. 220)

The following story illustrates what I am talking about.

There was a king who built a highway. He announced that when the highway was completed, he would hold a contest to see who could travel the road best. The winner would receive a grand prize.

On the appointed day, people came from far and near to travel the new highway. They wore jogging apparel, plain attire, or expensive clothing. Some brought chariots; others brought fine horses. Some brought partners; some had picnics along the way. They came in every different way possible as they traveled the king's highway. At the end of their travels, many of the people complained of a pile of rocks and debris left by the builders.

At the end of the day, there came a lone traveler along the highway. As he walked, he came to the pile of rocks and debris. He stopped and began to move them off the road. He moved small rocks of all sizes off the road. Eventually, he came to the last pile. As he lifted the final large rock out of its place, to his astonishment he found underneath it a pouch of gold.

He immediately took the gold to the king and said, "Your Majesty, I found this pouch of gold on the highway today as I was cleaning off a large pile of rocks and debris. I want to give it to you so you can return it to the rightful owner.

The king said, "You are the rightful owner."

The traveler said, "No, no. I have never known such wealth."

The king then said, "But you have won my contest—for he who

travels the road best is he who makes the road easier for those who follow." (Adapted from "King's Highway," in *Especially for Mormons*, vol. 2, p. 289, compiled by Stan and Sharon Miller. Provo: Kellirae Arts, 1973.)

When we are baptized, we make a sacred covenant. One of the things we promise to do is to be willing to mourn with those who mourn. At the waters of Mormon, Alma explained,

> And now, as ye are desirous to come into the fold of God, and to be called his people, and are willing to bear one another's burdens, that they may be light; Yea, and are willing to mourn with those that mourn;...
> (Mosiah 18:8-9)

In our relationships, do we really mourn with those who mourn? Do we comfort those who are in need of comfort? A woman I know who lost her husband shared how painful it was for her when, just a month after his death, there were people who told her to snap out of it and get on with her life.

Many of us think we know what is going on in the lives of those around us, but most of the time we know very little. People in our wards are going through trials of which we have no idea. A bishop once said to me, "If I could only lift the roofs off the homes in our ward and you could peek in and know what people are going through."

At one of the most challenging times in my life a woman in my ward said to me, "Diane, you are so lucky. Everything in your life is so perfect." I remember thinking, "If you only knew. . . ."

Let us not judge others. Some people cannot share their sorrows because doing so would hurt others. Let's remember the words of the hymn:

> Savior, may I love my brother
> As I know thou lovest me,
> Find in thee my strength, my beacon,

For thy servant I would be.
Savior, may I love my brother—Lord, I would follow
Thee. (Hymns, no. 220)

When I was in my later years of college, I was going through
another challenging time trying to decide whether to marry a particular young man. My parents were in Europe at that time, and
I remember coming home from work to an empty house.

I really needed to talk to someone. The first person who came
to mind was a dear friend by the name of John. He was a host on
Temple Square where I worked, and he was the kind of person I
could talk to about spiritual things. I could always communicate
with John spirit to spirit, but I remembered that he had a date
that night with one of my good friends. I thought, "I can't bother
John. Who else can I talk to?"

I went into my bedroom and got on my knees. I said,
"Heavenly Father, I am really struggling tonight. I need to talk to
somebody. I had hoped to talk with John, but he's on a date.
Heavenly Father, I know that thou dost care. Wilt *thou* listen to
me?" I talked to Heavenly Father about the things on my mind
and shared with him my feelings. Then I lay down on my bed,
fully clothed. I was so exhausted I fell asleep. I don't know how
long I was asleep—perhaps an hour.

The next thing I remember was a loud knocking on the front
door. When I opened the door, John and my girlfriend were
standing there. They were supposed to be on their date! John said,
"Is everything okay, Diane?"

I said, "How did you know . . . ?"

He said, "We are coming in to talk." They came in and sat
down, and the three of us talked about all the things that had been
troubling me. I am grateful for someone who was in tune with the
Spirit and listened to promptings.

The Holy Ghost can let us know what the Savior would have
us do.

I have found that it makes a real difference in my life if I pray every day that the Savior will let me know what people I can serve. As we listen carefully to the Spirit, there will be times throughout the month, the week, and the day that we will feel impressed to call someone or stop by for a visit.

President Harold B. Lee once commented that he would like to live his life so that the prayers of others may be answered through him. We need to have the same desire.

I will never forget an experience I had when I was a Relief Society president. We had no children yet, and I was working full-time for a computer company that was having some financial difficulties. One day they informed the employees that they were going out of business and would be closing their doors for good on Friday.

I knew I needed to find a new job, but I decided to devote my time to church work over the weekend. First thing Monday morning, I would find a Sunday newspaper and see if I could locate a job to apply for.

I woke up about five o'clock Monday morning and started to get ready to go out and buy a newspaper. At six o'clock, the telephone rang. It was a single mother with three children who had just moved to our ward from England. She was in a precarious situation. She had no money, no automobile, and no food in her house. She desperately needed help. She asked, "Could you please come and take me to the store to get some food for my family and then to register my children in school?" She had a list of needs that couldn't wait.

For a brief moment I struggled, thinking "I've got to go get a newspaper and get a job today." I knew what I should do, but I was torn. Names of several sisters in the ward raced through my mind—sisters whose families were raised, women who weren't working and had more time than I did. Any one of them would have been happy to help. However, the impression came firmly: "This one is yours."

I quickly said, "I would be happy to come help you. I will come as soon as I can get there." I hung up the phone and went into my bedroom, got on my knees, and asked Heavenly Father to help me do what he wanted me to do and to still be able to do what I needed to do.

Just as I was walking out the front door to leave, my neighbor was walking out her front door as well. In her arms was a huge stack of newspapers she was carrying to the garbage. I asked if she had the Sunday papers. My neighbor said, "Yes, do you want them?" I took them inside, quickly opened them up to the classified ads, and at a glance saw two positions that appealed to me. I circled them, closed the papers, and left.

It took most of the day to complete the list of errands my new friend needed help with. It was a joyful experience to become better acquainted with her and her children.

That afternoon when I came home, I opened up the newspapers and called about the positions I had underlined early that morning. It was getting late, but one of the businesses was still open. The position had not been filled yet, and, yes, I could come the next day to interview!

Within a few days I was hired for the position. I had never before had a job fall into place so perfectly. I knew I had received the blessing I had asked for. God always pours out a blessing if we seek first to do his will.

Several years later, while I was serving as the Beehive advisor in my ward, a young girl in my class was struggling with drugs and promiscuity. I was deeply concerned about her. At the time, I was traveling about the country speaking professionally.

I had a seminar that had to be written within a few weeks, and I was under tremendous pressure to get it done. I had a deadline coming up, and I still needed to do some research before I could write it.

I set a day aside to spend in the library gathering information. That morning when I woke up, the Spirit said, "Go and see Annie (not her real name). She needs your help today." I'm embarrassed to say that a battle went on inside me. I struggled in prayer, thinking, "Heavenly Father, please—I've got to do this research. Today is the only day I have . . . couldn't I go another day?" The feeling to visit Annie persisted. Finally I said, "I will go and help her, but Heavenly Father, wilt thou help me to somehow get this project done?"

I went to her home and spent the day with her. We bonded that day in a way we never had before, and I felt good about doing what I had been prompted to do. But the rest of the week was scheduled, and I didn't have any time to work on the seminar. I wondered when I could find time to do the sorely-needed research.

That Sunday as I walked into the foyer at church, Annette, a woman in our ward, came up to me and said, "Diane, wait right there—don't move! I have some things for you." I waited as she went out to her car. When she came back, she was juggling a stack of books and tapes about two feet high.

I said, "What are these?"

She said, "You need them, don't you?"

I looked at the titles on the books and tapes, and realized they were on the subject of the seminar I was writing. The titles were exactly what I needed to do my research for the seminar! I said, "I do! How did you know?"

She continued, "I had the most wonderful experience yesterday. While I was cleaning out my hallway closet, the impressions came: 'Diane needs that book, and that one and that one.'"

I stared at Annette, totally amazed! Feeling very humble, I said, "Thank you. You will never know how much it means to me that you were in tune with the Spirit." I realized how very much Heavenly Father is aware of us—of our time and our needs. He had saved me hours of searching to find the right books with the information I needed!

We are always indebted to him. He blesses our lives more than we can ever return to him. As we do our best to serve him, he keeps filling our cup with blessings.

Sometimes we get so focused on making money that we crowd out the more important relationships and ways we can give service. We believe we want to make money for righteous reasons, and we justify it by saying, "I want to make enough money so that I can be a mission president," or "I want to make enough money so that I can spend all of my time in the family history library," or "I want to make enough money so that I can help people in need." But what about *now*?

Not one of us is guaranteed that we will be alive tomorrow. What are we doing *today* to lift the kingdom, or to lift another? Jacob said it beautifully:

> But before ye seek for riches, seek ye for the kingdom of God.
>
> And after ye have obtained a hope in Christ ye shall obtain riches, if ye seek them; and ye will seek them for the intent to do good—to clothe the naked, and to feed the hungry, and to liberate the captive, and administer relief to the sick and afflicted. (Jacob 2:18-19)

Are we doing as Jacob counsels? As I see the lovely homes, boats, motor homes, condominiums, and other riches, I ask myself, "Are we using our abundance to build the kingdom of God?"

Certainly building our families and creating opportunities for family togetherness are a part of building the kingdom. What else might we do? Could we invite a nonmember family for a Saturday at the lake in our boat? Could we invite the missionaries to teach discussions in our lovely homes? Could we use some of the money we have to flood the earth with copies of the Book of Mormon? Could we take some of our fine apparel—not just that which is outgrown or worn out—to clothe the poor?

I am reminded of one family who heard of another family's financial need. They visited the other family's home while they were away and filled their kitchen cupboards, refrigerator, and pantry full of food just purchased at the grocery store. They also filled the freezer with frozen foods, and then quietly slipped away. The family returned, not knowing who had done this kindness, but feeling that there was a God in heaven who cared.

One woman I know who had been blessed financially became aware of another family who needed a car. She had two automobiles of her own. As an act of true kindness, she offered the use of one of her cars to the family who needed one. They were deeply moved by her act of compassion.

Another family lost their mother to cancer. The husband was overcome with grief. To add to the burden, he now had major medical bills to pay. Insurance had covered the largest portion, but they still had massive bills. Upon learning of this family's plight, someone anonymously sent checks to all the health care providers to pay the balances in full.

One gentleman pondered what he could do to serve others. As he thought about his talents, he realized he had a yard full of flowers. He went to a floral supply store and purchased vases. Each week, he cut flowers from his gardens and put them in a vase. He then took them to a neighboring nursing home, where he inquired at the front desk: "Who could use some cheering up?" Each week he would be directed to a different room. The staff and residents at the nursing home could count on his visits as he delivered the vases of beautiful flowers.

A family in one ward was pained and sorrowing because of something embarrassing and hurtful one of their family members had done. Some of the ward members snubbed them, but one neighbor showed Christlike love. She made a cake and showed up on their doorstep with her offering of love.

These acts exemplify the words of the scripture:

> Pure religion and undefiled before God and the Father is this, To visit the fatherless and widows in their affliction, and to keep himself unspotted from the world. (James 1:27)

Two missionaries who were companions at the Missionary Training Center decided they would do acts of kindness each day. During their free time they made cards and notes to leave anonymously by the doors of other missionaries who seemed to be having a difficult time or who were sad or discouraged. The cards cheered the other missionaries and showed them that someone cared.

The following poem expresses this philosophy well:

I knelt to pray as the day began
And prayed, "O God, bless every man.
Lift from each weary heart some pain
And let the sick be well again.
And then I rose to meet the day
And thoughtlessly went on my way;
I didn't try to dry a tear
Or take the time a grief to hear.
I took no steps to ease the load
Of hard-pressed travelers on the road;
I didn't even go to see
The sick friend who lives next door to me.

But then again when day was done
I prayed, "O God, bless everyone."
But as I prayed a voice rang clear
Instructing me to think and hear.
"Consult your own heart ere you pray:
What good have you performed today?
God's choicest blessings are bestowed
On those who help him bear the load."

And then I hid my face and cried,
"Forgive me, Lord, for I have lied.
Let me but live another day
And I will live it as I pray."

(Poem by Whitney Montgomery, quoted by Nicholas
G. Smith in *Conference Report,* April 1941, p. 127.
Used by permission.)

One Sunday morning I was getting ready to take my young
women with the other youth in my ward on the final day of our
super activity. We planned to help feed the homeless under a
viaduct in Salt Lake City.

As I got dressed early that Sunday morning, I felt cold and
reached for my favorite coat. We had been financially strapped for
several years, and I had been wearing my husband's old coat. My
mother had recently given me a brand-new, warm parka. I loved
it. It was my favorite color, and it was well insulated with a soft
flannel lining. I pulled the parka around me to keep in the
warmth. As I did so, my thoughts went elsewhere.

That morning, we would be going out into the cold to feed
the homeless. What if one of them didn't have a coat? I had never
considered that before. Here I was, standing inside my warm, cozy
home, cuddled in my beautiful coat. The people we would be visiting didn't have a home. What if they didn't have a coat, either?
That thought sent chills through me. I asked myself, "If I saw
someone this morning without a coat, would I be willing to give
them this one?"

Immediately I thought of all the reasons I shouldn't. I myself
had gone several years without a good coat. This coat was a gift
from my mother; I should never give a gift away. Besides that, it
might be too cold outside this morning for me to even take my
coat off. If I did so, I might freeze.

However, I knew I couldn't let someone without a home be
without a coat. I could always come home, where I could go
inside. Homeless people couldn't do that. I thought, "I know! I'll
go get my husband's old coat, the one I've been wearing for the
past few years, and wear it. Then if I see someone without a coat,
I can give them that one!"

Then I thought of the Savior. What would he do? Would he

give his second-best or worst? Or would he give his best? Tears filled my eyes. I knew in my heart what he would do. I also knew what I should do.

I watched the faces of the young men and women as we arrived at the viaduct. They looked shocked. Many of them had never seen people in such poverty. Some felt uncomfortable at first, but they seemed more at ease as they were put to work. They eagerly took their posts at each of the serving spots.

I guardedly looked around to see if there was a woman without a coat. There were only a few women, and they all had coats. *Whew!* I wouldn't have to give away my favorite coat after all!

Several hours later, just as we were getting ready to pack up and hurry home for church, I spotted a woman standing a short distance off who had on only a sweater.

I knew what God would have me do. I carefully took off my beautiful new parka, knowing I would not have a new coat myself for some time. I handed it to a couple of the young women in my class and asked them to take it over to that woman. They looked at me incredulously. "You want to give away this really good coat?" they asked.

When they left, I wept a few tears. I knew I had just given away something I truly valued. It wasn't the old coat I didn't wear anymore; it was something that meant a great deal to me. It was truly a gift of love to a stranger.

A few moments later, the young women returned. There were smiles on their faces as they told me what happened. They said as they approached the woman and asked if she would like the coat, she was overcome. She couldn't believe someone wanted to give her something so nice. She put the coat on and thanked them over and over. That cold morning, many important lessons were learned—especially by me.

As the Gulf War broke out in the Middle East, a young woman named Shellie was concerned when her mother was called to active duty as a nurse on the front line of battle. Shellie was a member of the Church; she had been converted, but her mother had not. Shellie struggled with the fact that her mother was on the front lines but had not yet been baptized into the Church.

One night shortly after her mother left, Shellie was sitting at home, hurting and struggling and praying, when the telephone rang. It was a young man who had felt impressed to call her. He said, "Are you okay?"

She said, "How did you know I was having a hard time tonight?"

He replied, "I was sitting at home, and I just had the feeling I should call and find out how you are."

That phone call let her know that Heavenly Father cared. Through the Spirit, he had inspired another person to be mindful of the pain Shellie was going through.

God will use us as instruments in his hands if we follow impressions when they come. When a name keeps going over and over in my mind, I have learned that I need to find out what that person needs that I am able to give. Sometimes it is only a phone call to let them know I am thinking of them; sometimes it is much more.

While I was pregnant with my second child, I became so sick the first few months that I could hardly keep my head up. It was in the fall of the year, during football season. Chris and I were avid BYU football fans, and for many years we had season tickets. We never missed a game, rain or shine.

One particular week of that season, Chris was especially excited. That Saturday BYU would be playing against its arch-rival, the University of Utah, in a home game!

Chris was excited all week long. On Saturday morning, we woke up early. He wanted to be on campus first thing so he could feel the electricity in the air. He said, "Come on, Diane, let's get going." I pulled myself out of bed and started getting ready, but I felt so sick I could tell I was not going to be able to go. I told Chris I thought I had better stay home in bed. "Is it okay if I go to the game?" he asked.

I smiled because he knew I would never make him miss *this*

game. Chris headed to Provo with his family, leaving me with our three-year-old. I went back to sleep and slept for about an hour. Then Whitney woke up and insisted, "Mommy, Mommy, come feed me. Mommy, I need you."

I pulled myself out of bed, but the nausea was so bad I kept wanting to double over. Tears started streaming down my face. I knew I needed help. Immediately I thought about calling my mother. She would have come in a second, but my sister-in-law was bedridden with her pregnancy, and Mom had been helping her. I thought, "She needs Mom more than I do today," so I didn't call.

I tried to think of who I could call on for help. All of my husband's family and the rest of my family were at the game. The names of several friends came to mind, but I didn't want to impose on their Saturday. I continued to wonder, "Who can I call?"

I went into my bedroom, knelt down, and prayed, "Dear Father in Heaven, I need help." I said, "I know that thou hast never been pregnant before, but I know in thine infinite wisdom thou dost understand how I am feeling right now." He did understand, because as I prayed, the telephone rang. I knew it was help. I said, "Thank you, Heavenly Father. That was really fast." It was my visiting teacher, Pat.

She said, "Hi, Diane. I was working around the house and kept thinking of you. Are you okay?"

I said, "I'm doing okay, but not great." Then the tears began to flow. I wasn't doing very well at all. We talked, and Pat got me laughing. She cheered me up as we talked and laughed for twenty minutes. Laughing magically helps any problem. Then she said, "Do you want me to come over?"

"I feel better already," I said. "I think I'll be all right." But as I hung up the phone, I realized I still needed help. At that moment there was a loud knock at the door. I thought, "Heavenly Father, thank you again." I knew it wasn't Pat, unless she had been standing outside the door with a cellular phone, but in my heart

I knew it was help.

I went to the door, opened it up, and saw my mother standing there. It was like seeing an oasis in the desert. She said, "Hi, honey. I woke up this morning and something inside said, 'Go and see Diane today, she needs you.'"

As we learn to ask, "Dear Father, whom wouldst Thou have me serve today?" we will find that serving others makes a great difference in their lives, as well as our own. The Lord will bless us as we serve him.

Chapter Seven

ACCEPTING THE ULTIMATE GIFT

Two thousand years ago in the Garden of Gethsemane, our elder brother, Jesus Christ, atoned for our sins. He gave of himself freely and selflessly so that you and I could have eternal life, the ultimate gift of love from the Father:

> For God so loved the world, that he gave his only begotten Son, that whosoever believeth in him should not perish, but have everlasting life.
>
> For God sent not his Son into the world to condemn the world; but that the world through him might be saved. (John 3:16-17)

God's work and glory is to bring to pass the immortality and eternal life of man (see Moses 1:39). We all clearly understood what this meant as we rejoiced in heaven upon learning of the plan of salvation. We looked forward to our own mortal probation, during which we could prove ourselves worthy to return to God's presence.

President Brigham Young elaborated on the redemption process:

> Jesus had been with his Father, talked with him, dwelt in his bosom, and knew all about heaven, about making the earth, about the transgression of man, and what would redeem the people, and that he was the character who was to redeem the sons of earth, and the earth itself from all sin that had come upon it. The light, knowledge, power, and glory with which he was clothed were far above or exceeded that of all others

who had been upon the earth after the fall. Consequently, at the very moment, at the hour, when the crisis came for him to offer up his life, the Father withdrew himself, withdrew his Spirit; and cast a veil over him. That is what made him sweat blood. If he had had the power of God upon him, he would not have sweat blood; but all was withdrawn from him and a veil was cast over him, and he then plead (sic) with the Father not to forsake him." (*Deseret News Weekly*, February 26, 1856, p. 402. Used by permission.)

And President Joseph Fielding Smith explained the twofold nature of the Atonement:

First, "By His death upon the cross, He redeemed all mankind from death."

Secondly, "He redeems all mankind from sin but only on condition of: faith in God, repentance from sin, and baptism by immersion—a burial in water for the remission of sins." (*Answers to Gospel Questions*, vol. 3. Salt Lake City: Deseret Book Company, 1976, p. 179.)

This gift is offered to all, but not all have yet received it. It is to let others know of this gift that the Church sends missionaries out into the world, maintains visitors' centers, and uses many other methods to acquaint all humankind with the message of the gospel of Jesus Christ.

In the late 1970s, I was a full-time hostess in the visitors' center on Temple Square in Salt Lake City. One of the volunteer hosts had a significant experience he shared with me at that time.

A nun of some importance and her entourage visited Temple Square, and my friend accompanied their VIP tour in the North Visitors' Center. In the first hall, they saw the statue of Adam and Eve and the large paintings depicting significant events in the lives of Old Testament prophets. The nun appeared to be moved as she looked at the paintings.

They then walked up the circular ramp into the rotunda, where Thorvaldsen's beautiful *Christus* is displayed. Again this woman, who had devoted her life to serving Christ, appeared to be deeply moved by what she saw.

Next, they moved up a few steps into the hallway where they saw paintings depicting the life of Jesus Christ.

The final room of the tour before entering the theater was the Restoration Room, which displayed a diorama of the Prophet Joseph Smith kneeling in the sacred grove. On the wall were quotes from early apostles and reformers who spoke of a falling away and a restoration of all things.

The message this woman now heard was contrary to everything she had devoted her life to. She did, however, continue with the tour and saw the film *Man's Search for Happiness.* Apparently the film had a tremendous positive effect on her, because at that point, she wept.

The theater provided shrink-wrapped copies of the Book of Mormon behind each seat. They were easily accessible for anyone who wanted to pick up a copy and purchase it after the film. The tour guide bore his testimony at the end of the tour, and the guests were invited to look around on their own. The nun picked up a copy of the Book of Mormon. She left the theater and there found my friend, the host. She handed him the book and asked him if he would tell her more about it. He sat down with her on a bench with the Book of Mormon in hand, and they ripped off the plastic wrapping around it.

In telling me the story he said, "As we opened that book, it fell open to a certain page. On that page, to my surprise, there was a scripture underlined." They looked at each other in astonishment, realizing that this was a new book from which they had just torn the plastic.

They read the underlined scripture:

> Wherefore, do the things which I have told you I
> have seen that your Lord and your Redeemer should
> do; for, for this cause have they been shown unto me,
> that ye might know the gate by which ye should enter.
> For the gate by which ye should enter is repentance
> and baptism by water; and then cometh a remission of
> your sins by fire and by the Holy Ghost. (2 Ne. 31:17)

As the nun read those words, she looked up at the host and
said, "What does this all mean?"

He said, "The Lord is trying to send a message to you. He
wants you to be baptized into his true church." Missionaries were
sent to teach the woman, and in a very short time she entered the
waters of baptism.

Most of us have already entered the gate of baptism, but have
we continued to do what we have been instructed to do? Let's read
on from that passage in 2 Nephi 31. Verses 19-20 state:

> And now, my beloved brethren, after ye have gotten
> into this strait and narrow path, I would ask if all is
> done? Behold, I say unto you, Nay; for ye have not
> come thus far save it were by the word of Christ with
> unshaken faith in him, relying wholly upon the merits
> of him who is mighty to save.
>
> Wherefore, ye must press forward with a steadfast-
> ness in Christ having a perfect brightness of hope, and
> a love of God and of all men. Wherefore, if ye shall
> press forward, feasting upon the word of Christ, and
> endure to the end, behold, thus saith the Father: Ye
> shall have eternal life.

In D&C 14:7 we read similar counsel: "And, if you keep my
commandments and endure to the end you shall have eternal life,

which gift is the greatest of all the gifts of God."

As we look back over the past few years, we can see that the number of prophesied events which have come to pass has been almost overwhelming—the fall of the Iron Curtain, allowing the spread of the gospel into many previously unopened areas of the earth; widespread wars and tumults; seasons changing; thunders; earthquakes; and devastating disease.

Are we living our lives in such a way that if the Savior does return in our lifetime, we will be prepared to meet him?

As we embrace the Atonement, we *can* endure our challenges in this life, and thus be able to embrace eternal life. It is offered to all but not embraced by all. It is the ultimate gift of love, and is given to all who qualify.

There are several ways we can prepare ourselves so we can embrace this ultimate gift of love.

Repentance

The first way to prepare ourselves for the gift of eternal life is through *repentance*. It is humbling when we understand that because of the Atonement, we can repent, be truly forgiven of any wrongdoing in our lives, and one day be able to stand before the Father, blameless and pure.

To use this wonderful gift he has given us, we need to make sure we are not too caught up in our daily routines to take the time to talk to Heavenly Father and ask forgiveness each day for our offenses. It is easy to see the faults of others and constantly find the motes in their eyes, but it is easier to overlook the beams in our own.

President Spencer W. Kimball once said that each night before he went to bed, he would plead with Heavenly Father to forgive him for anything he had done that day contrary to His will. I realized then that each night before going to bed, I too, must learn to plead for forgiveness.

The ancient prophet Nephi was great and much admired, but he, too, felt the need for repentance. He reflected,

> I am encompassed about, because of the temptations and the sins which do so easily beset me.
>
> And when I desire to rejoice, my heart groaneth because of my sins; nevertheless, I know in whom I have trusted.
>
> My God hath been my support; he hath led me through mine afflictions in the wilderness; and he hath preserved me upon the waters of the great deep. (2 Ne. 4:18-20)

When we are tempted, do we turn to prayer with a repentant heart and put our whole trust in God, as Nephi did?

President Kimball also stated: "When one has washed his robes in the blood of the Lamb, they are no longer soiled!" (Spencer W. Kimball, "A Letter to a Friend," pamphlet, p. 23. Salt Lake City: Church of Jesus Christ of Latter-day Saints, 1971. Used by permission.) And the scriptures tell us that "Though your sins be as scarlet, they shall be as wool" (Isa. 1:18).

A story that deeply touched my heart was given in a conference talk by Elder Vaughn J. Featherstone. He related an experience he had while he was a stake president:

> One day a woman came to my business office. She leaned across the desk and said, "President, I have carried a transgression on my heart for thirty-four years that I cannot carry one more step in this life, but I know how tender-hearted you are, and I wouldn't add one particle of a burden to your soul."
>
> I said, "My dear sister, before you go on, let me share with you a principle of the gospel. When you take a burden off your soul, it is lifted from the priesthood leader's soul also."

She said, "Thirty-four years ago, before my first husband and I were married, I was involved in an abortion. Since that time, I have felt like a murderess. It was my husband's idea, and I did not resist. I had an abortion. Later we got married. He was unfaithful constantly during the first two years of our marriage. I finally divorced him and have since married a wonderful man who is a convert to the Church. He knows everything, and he still wants to be sealed to me. President, do you think that either in time or in eternity we can be sealed together? I know I will be cast out, but does it have to be forever?" The tears flowed down her cheeks.

I had known this woman and thought she was one of the most Christlike women I had ever met. She always baked bread, rolls or cookies for the people in the neighborhood. Whenever they had a ward party and the Relief Society sisters cleaned up, she always scrubbed the floor. She explained she hadn't felt worthy to stand by them and do the dishes; she only felt worthy to scrub the floor where they walked. She told me she had never gossiped about anyone else. "How could I," she said, "after what I had done?"

I listened to her confession, humbled to tears, and told her, "I have never had a case of abortion before. I will need to write to President Kimball, President of the Quorum of the Twelve, and get his counsel."

I wrote to President Kimball and shared the entire story. I told him she was willing to submit to any decision he would have for her. Two weeks later I received his response. I called the sister and asked her to meet me at the stake office as soon as she could. When I arrived at the stake center, she was already there. Her eyes were red, and she was pale. I know she must have been on her knees after my call, asking for mercy.

Again I sat across the desk from her and said, "I do

not want to keep you waiting one second longer. We are not even going to stop for prayer. Let me read you President Kimball's letter.

'Dear President Featherstone: You inquired about a woman who had been involved in an abortion thirty-four years ago. From the way you describe her, it sounds like she has long since repented. You may tell her on behalf of the Church she is forgiven.

'After a thorough and searching interview, you may issue this sweet sister a temple recommend so she can go to the temple and be sealed to her present husband.'"

If the Savior had been sitting where the woman sat, I would not have felt any closer to him. I believe that is exactly what he would have done. It was as though a two-thousand-pound burden had been lifted from the heart of this good woman. She wept great tears of relief and joy. To this day, I do not remember who the woman was. ("Forgive Them I Pray Thee," *Ensign*, Nov. 1980, pp. 29-31. Used by permission.)

President J. Reuben Clark, Jr., said:

> I feel that [the Savior] will give that punishment which is the very least that our transgression will justify....
>
> I believe that when it comes time to make the rewards for our good conduct, he will give us the maximum that it is possible to give. (J. Reuben Clark, Jr., "As Ye Sow...," Provo, Utah: Brigham Young University Speeches of the Year, May 3, 1955, p. 7)

What a wonderful gift *repentance* is!

Elder Vaughn J. Featherstone shared another story of a young man who learned the value of repentance:

Shortly after I had been called to the Presiding Bishopric, an Arizona stake president told me he had a young missionary candidate who needed to be interviewed for worthiness...

As I invited the young man into my office, . . . I said to him:

"Apparently there has been a major transgression in your life...Would you mind being very frank and open and telling me what that transgression was?"

With head held high and in a haughty manner he responded,"'There isn't anything I haven't done."

I responded: "Well, then, let's be more specific. Have you been involved in fornication?"

Very sarcastically, he said, "I told you I've done everything..."

I said, "I would to God your transgression was not so serious."

"Well, it is," he replied.

"How about drugs?"

"I told you I've done everything."

Then I said, "What makes you think you're going on a mission?"

"Because I have repented," he replied. "I haven't done any of those things for a year. I know I'm going on a mission because my patriarchal blessing says I'm going on a mission. I've been ordained an elder. I've lived the way I should this past year, and I know that I'm going on a mission."

I looked at the young man sitting across the desk; twenty-one years old, laughing, sarcastic, haughty, with an attitude far removed from sincere repentance. And I said to him: "My dear young friend, I'm sorry to tell you this, but you're not going on a mission. Do you suppose we could send you out with your braggadocio attitude about this past life of yours, boasting of your escapades? Do you think we could send you out with the fine, clean young men who have never violated the moral code, who have kept their lives clean and pure and worthy so that they might go on missions? . . .

"What you have committed is a series of monumental transgressions," I continued. "You haven't repented; you've just stopped doing something. Someday, after you have been to Gethsemane and back, you'll understand what true repentance is."

At this the young man started to cry. He cried for about five minutes, and during that time I didn't say a word...I just sat and waited as this young man cried.

Finally he looked up and said, "I guess I haven't cried like that since I was five years old."

I told him: "If you had cried like that the first time you were tempted to violate the moral code you may well have been going on a mission today. Now, I'm sorry, I hate to be the one to keep you from realizing your goal. I know it will be hard to go back to your friends and tell them you are not going on a mission.

"After you've been to Gethsemane," I continued, "you'll understand what I mean when I say that every person who commits a major transgression must also go to Gethsemane and back before he is forgiven."

The young man left the office, and I'm sure he wasn't very pleased; I had stood in his way and kept him from going on a mission. About six months later, I was in Arizona speaking at the Institute at Tempe. After my talk many of the Institute members came down the aisles to shake hands. As I looked up I saw this young man—the non-repentant transgressor—coming down the aisle toward me. . . .

I reached down to shake hands with him, and as he looked up at me, I could see that something wonderful had taken place in his life. Tears streamed down his cheeks. An almost holy glow came from his countenance. I said to him, "You've been there, haven't you?"

And through tears he said, "Yes, Bishop Featherstone, I've been to Gethsemane and back."

"I know," I said. "It shows in your face. I believe now that the Lord has forgiven you."

He responded: "I'm more grateful to you than you'll ever know for not letting me go on a mission. It would have been a great disservice to me. Thanks for helping me." (*A Generation of Excellence*, Salt Lake City: Bookcraft, 1975, pp.156-59.)

The Lord has said:

Therefore I command you to repent—repent, lest I smite you by the rod of my mouth, and by my wrath, and by my anger, and your sufferings be sore—how sore you know not, how exquisite you know not, yea, how hard to bear you know not.

For behold, I, God have suffered these things for all, that they might not suffer if they would repent;

But if they would not repent they must suffer even as I;

Which suffering caused myself, even God, the greatest of all, to tremble because of pain, and to bleed at every pore, and to suffer both body and spirit—and would that I might not drink the bitter cup, and shrink—

Nevertheless, glory be to the Father, and I partook and finished my preparations unto the children of men.

Wherefore, I command you again to repent, lest I humble you with my almighty power; and that you confess your sins, lest you suffer these punishments of which I have spoken, of which in the smallest, yea, even in the least degree you have tasted at the time I withdrew my Spirit. (D&C 19:15-20)

Forgiveness

A second way we can prepare ourselves to embrace the ultimate gift of love goes hand in hand with repentance. It is the ability and the desire to *forgive.* There is nothing that will canker the soul more than not being able to forgive those who have transgressed against us.

Elder Hugh W. Pinnock tells the story of a woman who came to him for a health blessing. She had been sick for many years. She had changed doctors more than annually because of her illness, but her health was no better.

After he listened to this woman tell him of her problems, Elder Pinnock refused to give her a health blessing. He felt inspired to tell her that the problem hurting her was not physical, but emotional. Her emotional turmoil was manifesting itself in her health.

In the course of their interview, Elder Pinnock learned that the woman's husband had not treated her very well seven years earlier, and she had never forgiven him.

"You mean this sickness could be caused by unforgiveness?" she inquired.

Elder Pinnock gave her a blessing that she would be able to forgive her husband. She came to Elder Pinnock later and told him that she had been able to forgive him, and she now felt better than she had in years. Forgiveness does heal.

I have a wonderful sister who is a few years older than me. She had, I believe, one of the happiest and most satisfying marriages of anyone I have known. Karen and Bruce were deeply devoted to each other all their married life. She was a good wife to him, supporting him in many Church callings, including serving in a bishopric, then as a bishop and as a member of a stake presidency for many years. In the midst of busy Church service, he started a new business that demanded much of his time. But I never heard Karen complain. She always said, "I can endure any trial in this life as long as Bruce is by my side."

One morning in 1990, Karen and Bruce and their children, ages four years to seventeen, arose early, as was their custom. They gathered in the living room for their morning devotional. They read the scriptures together and then knelt down in family prayer. After prayer, they gave each other hugs and each went to get ready for the day.

In the early afternoon, Karen was talking with two of her teenagers when the phone rang. Karen answered it, and the teenagers knew by the look on her face that something was dreadfully wrong. They said, "Mom what's wrong?"

"Your dad's been shot . . . " The caller had informed Karen that her husband was in serious condition and was on his way to LDS Hospital in a Life Flight helicopter. He told her to get to the emergency room at the hospital as soon as possible and to have a neighbor bring her. Her three older children said, "We are going!" The immediate thought that came into her mind was, "What are you going to do without him?" She brushed it off, thinking, "Bad thought, bad thought." Karen then fell to her knees and pleaded with Heavenly Father to make everything all right.

The thirty-minute ride to the hospital was silent. All the way she prayed, "Please let him live, let him live." When they arrived, Karen and her children were immediately escorted into a small room. There, Karen learned that her beloved husband of nineteen years was dead. He was gone . . . gone.

As her seventeen-year-old son heard the news, he crumpled into a ball on the floor, crying, "Not my dad, not my dad, not my dad!" Her fifteen-year-old hysterically cried, "No, no, what are we going to do?" Her twelve-year-old went into denial and said, "We don't know that it's Dad; we haven't seen him yet." Within minutes they were allowed to see the body. It was Bruce . . . and Karen's heart literally broke.

I cannot express in words the sorrow this family has endured.

No words in the English language can sufficiently describe their loss.

I share this tender story with you because of how my sister handled her feelings. In her anguish, she visited the temple often, sought priesthood blessings, read the scriptures, and prayed with a broken heart and a contrite spirit for the Lord to help her with continued peace of mind. God heard her pleas, and she felt over-whelming comfort.

Karen easily forgave the man who took the life of her hus-band. She has no hate in her heart for the person who inflicted this great burden of sorrow upon her and her children. She still misses her sweetheart; but because of the forgiveness in her heart, Karen has been healed from the devastation of this loss. Her spirit shines bright.

Hanging on to hatred or a grudge and not letting go of some hurt in the past only hurts us. When we are unable to forgive those who have transgressed against us, our spiritual progress is curtailed.

Elder Marion D. Hanks has said, "I have felt that the ultimate form of love for God and men is forgiveness" (*Ensign*, January 1974, p. 20). And, at the end of his life, the Savior spoke words that will ring down through history: "Father, forgive them; for they know not what they do" (Luke 23:34).

As we forgive others and remove hate, anger, and disappoint-ment from our hearts, we prepare ourselves to receive eternal life.

Gratitude

A third way to prepare ourselves to embrace the gift of the Atonement is through *gratitude*. Honestly feeling gratitude in our hearts for all that God has done for us is a sign of spiritual strength.

A friend told me that just before her mission, her stake presi-dent shared with her how grateful the Lord was that she would go on a mission. He told her that the Lord would greatly bless her efforts in the mission field, and she would see many who would be receptive to the message of the gospel. "But remember," he said, "it is not because of you they will join the Church. It is because of the witness of the Holy Ghost. Always remember to give the credit to God. Express your gratitude to him often."

When she arrived in the mission field, she remembered her stake president's wise counsel. Every time she had an opportunity to teach someone, she and her companion would find a private area, behind a tree or at the side of a building, where they could bow their heads and offer a prayer of gratitude for the blessing of being able to teach an individual or a family about the gospel.

Many tender prayers were offered. She said she was always amazed at how soon after they had expressed feelings of gratitude they would be blessed with a new contact, especially since she was in an area where missionaries had a difficult time finding people to teach, and an even more difficult time finding people willing to enter the waters of baptism.

It seemed that the more they offered thanks, the more Heavenly Father blessed their efforts. After each prayer of gratitude, they would be guided to another person to teach.

One day while she and her companion were working with the elders in their district, the missionaries became discouraged because they were having no luck. She suggested that they go to a private spot and offer a prayer of thanks. The elders were willing. Together they raised their voices to heaven, expressing gratitude for their blessings as missionaries.

Then they went back to tracting. As they moved up the stairs in a large apartment complex, one of the elders stopped and said, "We need to stop at this door."

They stopped and knocked. A woman opened the door. For a brief moment she hesitated, then she invited the group of missionaries in. Within two months that dear woman was baptized.

King Benjamin knew the importance of gratitude: "And behold also, if I, whom ye call your king, who has spent his days in your service, and yet has been in the service of God, do merit any thanks from you, O how you ought to thank your heavenly King!" (Mosiah 2:19). And the Doctrine and Covenants tells us that "In nothing doth man offend God, or against none is his wrath kindled, save those who confess not his hand in all things, and obey not his commandments" (D&C 59:21).

Acknowledging the hand of God in our lives and pouring out thanks to him is essential to our progress in this life, and to our attainment of eternal life.

Attending the Temple

Another way to prepare ourselves for eternal life is by preparing ourselves to be worthy for a temple recommend and then attending the temple often. President Spencer W. Kimball said:

> All through Europe the past five months I have been encouraging the Saints to prepare their lives and put their houses in order and find the way to the holy temple. I told them in Germany the other day, "You can go to the temple." I knew their poverty and some of them, I knew, would have difficulty going. And then I said to them, as they had a look of questioning in their faces, "You could walk to the holy temple." There was a little laughter, . . . And then I said, "I am not facetious. You could all walk to the holy temple and it wouldn't be nearly as far as many of our ancestors walked to go to a place where there was not a temple, but where there was a barren, desert ground on which a temple could be built, and then they worked forty years to build the temple so they might enjoy all these privileges." I am sure that they do not fully understand yet, nor can they until they have come and tasted of its sweet spirit. (*The Teachings of Spencer W. Kimball*, Edward L. Kimball, ed. Salt Lake City: Bookcraft, 1988, pp. 535-536.)

A few years ago I was upset with someone who had wronged me, and I was hurting. To make matters worse, a few weeks later I received news of some wonderful things that were happening in this person's life. It hurt even more to think that such good things could happen to someone who had been so unkind to me.

The day I received that news I was struggling. Whatever I tried to do, I couldn't get it off my mind. I knew I needed to go to the temple to rid myself of these negative feelings.

As I prepared myself to go, I realized I didn't feel worthy to be in the temple. The reason I needed to go was the very reason I didn't feel worthy to go. However, I continued to get ready, and made arrangements for my children to be taken care of while I was gone.

While I drove the twenty-minute distance, I pleaded with Heavenly Father to help me forgive the person who had wronged me. As I poured out my heart in prayer, an interesting thing happened. Heavenly Father opened up my mind to recall past events in my own life. Vividly present in my mind were times in my life when I had knowingly or unknowingly been unkind to others. One by one, I had a bright recollection of the thoughtless acts I had inflicted on others.

Gradually, my prayer changed from one of pleading to be able to forgive someone else to one of humbly asking forgiveness for wrongs I had done. By the time I arrived at the temple, my heart had softened toward the person who had hurt me. I realized that perhaps in her heart she had not meant to be unkind.

The negative feelings that troubled me that day left because of my desire to go to the temple and to feel worthy to be there. While I was in the Lord's house, feelings of love and forgiveness welled up inside me.

Within a few weeks the person called to apologize, expressing how difficult the situation had been for her. She made complete recompense for the wrong that had been done.

In April of 1987, Elder Vaughn J. Featherstone offered a beau-

tiful Temple Statement for the Utah South Area. I would like to
share a few excerpts from that statement:

> The season of the world before us will be like no
> other in the history of mankind. Satan has and will
> unleash every evil, every scheme, every blatant vile per-
> version ever known to man in any generation. Just as
> this dispensation is the fulness of times, so it is also the
> dispensation of the fulness of evil. We and our wives or
> husbands, our children, and our members must find
> safety. There is no safety in the world; wealth cannot
> provide it, enforcement agencies cannot assure it,
> membership alone in this Church will not guarantee it.
>
> As the evil night darkens upon this generation, we
> must come to the temple for light and safety. In our
> temples we find quiet, sacred havens where the storm
> cannot penetrate to us. Unseen sentinels oftentimes
> watch over us. The Prophet Joseph pled with God dur-
> ing the dedicatory prayer at Kirtland: "And we ask
> thee, Holy Father, that Thy servants may go forth from
> this house [temple] armed with Thy power and that
> Thy name may be upon them and Thine Angels have
> charge over them." The Lord has promised, "For I will
> go before your face. I will be on your right hand and
> on your left, and my Spirit shall be in your hearts, and
> mine angels round about you, to bear you up" (D&C
> 84:88). Surely angelic attendants guard the temples of
> the most high God. It is my conviction that as it was
> in the days of Elisha, so it will be for us. "They that be
> with us are more than they that be with them" (2 Kings
> 6:16).
>
> Before the Savior comes the world will darken.
> There will come a time when even the elect will begin
> to lose hope if they do not come to the temples. The
> world will be so filled with evil that the righteous will

only feel secure through their faith in Christ and within the temple walls. I believe the Saints will come to the temples not only to do vicarious work but also to find a God-given haven of peace. The true and faithful Latter-day Saints will long to bring their children to our temples for safety's sake.

The Lord has promised that He will "suddenly come to His temple" (D&C 36:8). "The day or the hour no man knoweth; but it surely shall come" (D&C 39:21). We need to prepare for that day. There are some who will sit in the Quorum of the Twelve Apostles living among us today. They will be continuously called over the years and many of us are walking with them not knowing that one day God will move His hand and the mantle of apostleship will rest upon them. Others in our homes and communities throughout the world will receive apostolic callings. We must keep them sweet, clean, and pure in an oh-so-wicked world. Mothers will cradle in their arms and nurse at their bosoms babes who have been foreordained to be the living oracles of God.

There will be greater hosts of unseen beings in the temple. Joseph told the brethren, "And I beheld that the temple was filled with angels" (*History of the Church*, vol. 2, p. 428). I believe prophets of old as well as those in this dispensation will visit the temples. Those who attend the temple will feel their strength and companionship. We will not be alone in our temples. (From an address originally delivered in April 1987. Revised version later published privately by Elder Vaughn J. Featherstone. Also published in *Holiness to the Lord*, Salt Lake City: Deseret Book Company, 1994 edition, p. 1. Used by permission.)

There are many who have had their most sacred experiences in the temple. It is there that heaven seems only a whisper away. I have found that when I attend the temple, not only is my day filled with peace, but I am a better person, a more compassionate mother, a more giving neighbor, and a kinder friend.

As we come from the temple, our families and associates will feel the sweeter spirit that emanates from us. As we seek to go to the temple often, we will find the peace we need in these days of trial, to endure to the end and prepare us for eternal life.

The Second Comforter

One of the greatest promises given to us is that of being able to receive the Second Comforter. The Prophet Joseph Smith gave these instructions to the Twelve in 1839:

> After a person has faith in Christ, repents of his sins, and is baptized for the remission of his sins and receives the Holy Ghost (by the laying on of hands), which is the first Comforter, then let him continue to humble himself before God, hungering and thirsting after righteousness, and living by every word of God and the Lord will soon say unto him, "Son, thou shalt be exalted." When the Lord has thoroughly proved him, and finds that the man is determined to serve Him at all hazards, then the man will find his calling and his election made sure, then it will be his privilege to receive the other Comforter, which the Lord hath promised the Saints, as is recorded in the testimony of St. John, in the 14th chapter. (Marion G. Romney quoting Joseph Smith, Conference Report, October 1965, p. 21. Used by permission.)

Just thirteen months before his martyrdom, on May 14, 1843, and again on May 21, 1843, Joseph Smith exhorted the Saints to make their calling and election sure:

. . . They then would want that more sure word of prophecy, that they were sealed in the heavens and had the promise of eternal life in the kingdom of God. Then, having this promise sealed unto them, it was an anchor to the soul, sure and steadfast. Though the thunders might roll and lightnings flash, and earth-quakes bellow, and war gather thick around, yet this hope and knowledge would support the soul in every hour of trial, trouble and tribulation. (Ibid.)

God is totally aware of us individually. A few years ago, while praying for the blessing of the Second Comforter, I was impressed to open my scriptures. They fell open and my eyes came to rest upon this verse:

Therefore, sanctify yourselves that your minds become single to God, and the days will come that you shall see him; for he will unveil his face unto you, and it shall be in his own time, and in his own way, and according to his own will. (D&C 88:68)

My heart was moved as I read, for I knew that God was aware of the desires of my heart.

God knows that we are in the midst of trials, troubles, and tribulation as the world darkens. Yet he also sees the big picture. He knows the beauty, the love, and the peace that will be given to those who endure. To receive that comfort, we must do as the scriptures tell us:

Wherefore, ye must press forward with a steadfast-ness in Christ, having a perfect brightness of hope, and a love of God and of all men. Wherefore, if ye shall press forward, feasting upon the word of Christ, and endure to the end, behold, thus saith the Father: Ye shall have eternal life. (2 Ne. 31:20)

The Doctrine and Covenants tells us that ". . . Ye shall have eternal life, which gift is the greatest of all the gifts of God" (D&C 14:7). Further, we are given this comforting assurance: "Behold, he that hath eternal life is rich" (D&C 6:7).

May we all strive to live worthy of that great blessing, turning our hearts and our lives to Him who made eternal life possible. May we all "Trust in the Lord."